NICKY HASLAM
A DESIGNER'S LIFE

AN ARCHIVE OF INSPIRED DESIGN AND DÉCOR

NICKY HASLAM
A DESIGNER'S LIFE
AN ARCHIVE OF INSPIRED DESIGN AND DÉCOR

New York · Paris · London · Milan

First published in the United States
of America in 2015 by
Rizzoli International Publications, Inc.
300 Park Avenue South
New York, NY 10010
www.rizzoliusa.com

Originally published in 2014 by
Jacqui Small LLP
An imprint of Aurum Press Ltd
74–77 White Lion Street
London N1 9PF

2015 2016 2017 2018 / 10 9 8 7 6 5 4 3 2 1

ISBN: 978-0-8478-4509-5

Library of Congress Control Number:
2014948331

Printed in China

PUBLISHER Jacqui Small

SENIOR EDITOR Claire Chandler

COMMISSIONING AND PROJECT EDITOR
Zia Mattocks

ART DIRECTION AND DESIGN Paul Tilby

PICTURE RESEARCH Karen Howes/The
Interior Archive

PRODUCTION Maeve Healy

Contents

Sketch of an entrance to a *mas* in France *(page 1)*. A dining room in a country house in Hampshire *(page 2)*. My drawing room in London *(page 3)*. The design scheme for the room shown on pages 174–5 *(pages 4–5)*. In the garden at the Hunting Lodge *(pages 6–7)*. In front of the fire in London *(page 9)*. My dining table, set for an intimate dinner *(page 10)*.

INTRODUCTION

For nearly fifty years my lifeblood has been houses, buildings, rooms, gardens; what and who they contain; where and why people go into them, and how and when they are used; whether they are uplifting, surprising, calming, newly built or a ruin, modern or classic, charming muddles or staggering statements of style or power, or whispered, exemplary refinement. Personal taste, in all its variations—the eccentric, the grand gesture, the flamboyant, the simple, and often the downright hilarious—is grist to my visual mill. It always was, it always will be.

Having taste, by which I mean the love of whatever pleases us, and whatever we are comfortable with, is its basic form; but a discrimination, an innate desire to choose what we're surrounded by and gives pleasure to others, is different. We all know people who go "Yuck," on seeing plastic chair-covers, as well as those who say "I wouldn't give it house-room," when shown furniture by Riesener or Vardy. Both views are totally valid. Our "taste" is inherent. But taste's bigger brother, style, comes with inquisitiveness, imagination, audacity, a sense of history, an urge to redefine and reinterpret. Taste is inert, style is proactive.

These two themes kept recurring as I planned this book. I have seen and loved rooms that were the first, idiosyncratic and unchanging; and I have tried to make rooms that are the second. The joy of my particular profession is the range that this encompasses. A room or design doesn't have to be rich, gaudy, or resolutely plain, but somehow, somewhere, it should have the added fillip that makes it special and pleasurable to the eye. There are, I'm sure, examples in this book for the

"yuckers" and the "chuckers." But it's a highly personal overview, more a pictorial diary—scrapbook, even—than glacially cold perfection, reflecting the changes and underlining the constants of my long journey through the corridors and ballrooms of life. And I hope some of it, at least, will give pleasure to the eye and amusement to the memory, mingled, maybe, with an echo of nostalgia for the past and even, perhaps, a spark of inspiration for the future.

A multitude of people have influenced, inspired, and educated me. Many, whom memory brings to mind, are mentioned in this book, though given memory's fallibility, there are, of course, some glaring omissions. However arbitrarily, in daydreams the mind replays certain scenes, revisits evocative sights, tunes in to long-ago conversations, or conjures beloved faces. Yet the plain fact is that no phantom chisel is at hand with which to engrave those moments, the view or the voices, indelibly onto the slate of recollection. They drift and whisper in the ether. To all those overlooked, I can only give assurance that it's not for lack of trying, or love, or gratitude.

Much the same problem occurs when assessing all those whose support, succor, and creativity I have depended on since the early years of finally becoming involved in what I'd always subconsciously been drawn to—the substantiality and character of houses, buildings, rooms, and their appearance, contents, and livability. First and foremost of these is Flora Connell, without whose care, strength, advice, and humor I can barely function. Colette van den Thillart, Jena Quinn, Lucy Derbyshire, Molly Miller Mundy, Ethan Paramesh, and, until recently, Beata Heuman, have been my keystones for well over a decade, all of them unfazed by last-minute, long-haul flights for 24-hour meetings, or weeks billeted in dingy hotels from Moscow to Memphis. And in the past, such now-famed tycoons as Cath Kidston, Kirsty Allsopp, William Yeoward, Tom Bell, and Adam Sykes added laughter and luster to some stress-inducing situations.

The artists and craftsmen—essentially one and the same—who have turned my fumbling sketches, imprecise ideas, and mere notions into gloriously visual realities are legion. My admiration for the genius of Paul Czainski—who, with his first wife Janet, and now with Chris, his second, can transform builder's finish into magic marble, a blank wall into 3D, ceilings into jeweled coffering or star-scattered heavens, or dull wood into glowing amber—knows no bounds. Anyone from his "school,"

Lizzie Porter or Max Mouat among them, has the same flawless technique, as indeed does Karen Morris and her tireless team.

My passion for plasterwork has been indulged by Clark and Fenn (formerly the legendary Jacksons, their eighteenth-century trove of molds once housed in vast, white-dust-deep hangers in Hammersmith), dear, now-dead Rex from Designed Plastercraft, and Locker & Riley. Nicholas Gifford-Mead invariably has the perfect fire surround. Bill Schilling of Kaizen Furniture has created the most exquisite cabinetry, its quality echoed in furniture by Thomas Messel and Rupert Bevan. Steve Barnes of Tones has hung precious wallpapers, both David Turner and David Butler have fashioned unique light sources, and Nominka d'Albanella has incorporated pearls and butterfly wings into her astonishing *verres églomisés*. The buildings they all transform have frequently been completed by Andy Langridge, whose firm, Chelsea Construction, I've known since its inception; Christopher Butterworth, with his original eye, immense knowledge, and sense of scale, is always a coveted source and guide for antiques and objects to enhance them. These few are but drops in the ocean of ingenuity, receptiveness, and capability I have encountered over the years.

My further gratitude goes to my publisher, Jacqui Small; to my encouraging and tireless editor, Zia Mattocks; to Karen Howes for her tenacious picture research; to Claire Chandler and Maeve Healy at Jacqui Small LLP; and to Paul Tilby, whose cool brilliance this book owes its delectable appearance. Finally, I must express my deepest thanks to the owners of the rooms on its pages, and, above all, to Jonathan Newhouse and Nicholas Coleridge of Condé Nast Publications Inc., for their generous permission to reproduce so many photographs of my work, which originally appeared in that company's many magazines devoted to the most fascinating of subjects, interior design.

Nicky Haslam

FOUNDATIONS

I had a wildly varied bunch of parental forebears. My mother's lineage was largely Whig politicians or Georgian flibbertigibbets—profligate Georgiana, Duchess of Devonshire, and reckless Caroline Lamb, forever romantically associated with Lord Byron, were her great-great aunts—and many were famous as cricket players. My father came from a long line of solid Lancashire industrialists, and while his brothers became amateur architects, theater designers, and inventors, he was essentially business oriented. So I inherited a mixed bag of character traits, though from pretty early on it was clear I wasn't going in the political, sporting, or commercial direction. That left the artistic side as the foundation of my future, which, after flowing in diverse directions, settled on the pleasurable career explored in this book.

Early and Lasting Impressions

Not long ago, by chance, I happened to hear an abridged version of *Hamlet* on the radio. I'm not really up on Shakespeare, finding all but the most stylish performances mildly embarrassing. But that afternoon, sitting in a traffic jam, I found myself riveted by this simply spoken version, free from gesture and histrionics; and, unexpectedly, I heard a phrase that is not, as far as I know, a banal quotation. It struck me as something crucial to adolescence: "youth and observation."

The house where I was born *(above)*, Great Hundridge Manor in Buckinghamshire, looking exactly as I remember it. My father added the buildings on the right, joining the main block—a perfect William and Mary "box"—to the thirteenth-century chapel, and converted the farm buildings and barn into a nursery wing. *Country Life* magazine photographed the house during the Second World War *(opposite)*. The chinoiserie-paneled, faux-marbleized parlor, painted *c*1680, was, in reality, never as grimly tidy as it appears here.

Piccadilly, Manchester, before World War II from a drawing by L. S. Lowry, A.R.A.

THE SOCIETY OF DILETTANTI

This portrait of my mother Diana *(opposite, top left)*, painted by Robin Guthrie in 1950 and shown at the Royal Academy that year, hangs— appropriately, as she loved a martini —above the drinks tray at the Hunting Lodge, my "folly" in Hampshire. Shown next to it is a picture by Luke Sullivan of Bessborough House, a family home overlooking Richmond Park, designed by Sir William Chambers in the 1760s. I found the

picture in a Sotheby's sale, and soon after, the actual house—now part of Roehampton University and called Parkstead House—by climbing a high wall one evening. Mother's forebears, the Ponsonbys, were founders of the Dilettanti Society, whose portraits were painted for their club, Brooks's in St James's; my father's were, more prosaically, from a long line of cotton spinners in Lancashire, as the hoarding in this etching, by his friend

L. S. Lowry, of Manchester's Piccadilly Circus attests *(opposite, below)*. *The Parlour by Firelight*, as the artist John Hookham titled it, shows my parents changed into evening dress for dinner, despite the war *(above)*. The room has been a constant influence, and showed me the importance of light creating dramatic shadows. It was stripped of its exquisite paintwork by subsequent owners, but I've used it as inspiration a couple of times.

When my father found Hundridge, it was a ramshackle farm, but with the seventeenth-century house and its painted rooms miraculously unaltered. In one of these *(opposite)*, I lay for several childhood years with polio during the disease's last pre-Salk epidemic. Again, *Country Life* photographers made it look tidily comfortless, but it was warm and welcoming, and I got to know and love every grain of its fantasy marbleizing. The author Geoffrey Scott, with whom my father, a diplomat, shared digs in Rome (in the rooms that had been Keats's, with that sublime view of the Spanish Steps), had decorated Villa I Tatti in Florence for their friend Bernard Berenson, and so my father asked him to do the interior furnishings at Hundridge. Geoffrey's taste veered toward the simpler lines of the baroque, but my mother bamboozled him into a slightly more Frenchified style for her bedroom *(left)*. The balloon-like shape of the canopy was fascinating to stare up into on the rare occasions I shared her breakfast-in-bed tray.

Most of us are born with the power of observation. Whether we develop it is down to ourselves, whatever our situation. If we also have a dollop of retentive memory, so much the better. In my case, I was somehow blessed with the gift to grasp, early on, the form and color of things—and people—around me. Throughout the course of life, these things have continued to sink in, delight, and influence me; and it all began with a journey. It was quite short, and there were far longer and lovelier—and some less lovely—journeys to come, but this one was made repeatedly for a while and the memory of it, and the things I saw on it, remains clear.

My father had converted part of some huge, ancient barns, the creosote-blackened façades of which ringed the farmyard adjacent to the mellow brick house, into nursery quarters for his growing family. My two elder brothers, Michael and John, had long since progressed to bedrooms in the house; but, still a tot, I had to steel myself each morning to make this journey—not long, as I say, though in a child's eyeline endless—up the sloping corridor that joined the barns to the house.

There were cold, high windows on one side, shrouded with blackout material—it was wartime—and narrow shelves below; on the other, dark-framed prints and

"The pretty fire basket is now in my sitting room in the country. I buy an original whenever I see one; the modern copies are too small."

"This room, my father's bedroom, was always supposed to be haunted, but I never saw the ghost."

pictures on white walls, then the battened door of my mother's studio, more pictures, then a door to the servants' sitting room, and distantly, at the top, shafts of pale light from the kitchen window. I wasn't fearful—fear came later, when I had been told about ghosts and wolves. What I saw, each time more vividly, became imprinted on my conscience, and gradually I took in more of my surroundings. Having been created for my parents by a trio of great designers of their time, the house in which I lived certainly sent a visual message to my young eyes.

This training, if that's the word, continued as I began to recognize the actual beauty—and even ugliness—of things, later often accompanied by a desire to

The painting *(above left)*, by John Hookham, shows my father's bedroom before Geoffrey Scott had installed the baroque four-poster bed *(above right)*. My mother's room was almost unique for the 1920s for having an en-suite bathroom, but my dad had to trundle along a landing to his bathroom, a sink tucked into a cubbyhole in his bedroom, then considered all a man needed.

alter and improve them. Being blessed with a photographic visual memory and, for that matter, an aural one, too, I can still recall myriad rooms, see the people in them and hear the echo of what was spoken. That became useful as I grew closer to adulthood. Until then, I was fairly scatterbrained, spurred by whims, following goose-chase paths. Something seen, suggested, or overheard would set me off in a new direction: not for nothing were my mother's forebears founding members of the Dilettanti Society. As a young child, I had free rein to explore the woods and valleys surrounding the house, and a minimum of formal education beyond reading and writing, and not much arithmetic. Getting polio when I was seven put a stop to conventional schooling for several years. As a teenager, I began dabbling in drawing and painting, theater and fashion design. Decoration, as we now know it, was not on the cards. It was something that *had* been done in the past, and my parents made sure I witnessed many marvelous examples of it, but it wasn't until

The inspiration for the bed that Geoffrey Scott had made —starting quite a fashion for them —came from Carpaccio's *Dream of St Ursula* (1495), in the Gallerie dell' Accademia, Venice (*above*).

I saw the astonishing Diaghilev exhibition in London in 1954 that I observed that one could, even at that time, make spaces beautiful. From then on, the future seemed, if not exactly clear, at least imaginable.

Quite soon after, while still at school, I had the great fortune of meeting someone, quite by accident, who would catapult me into an adult world of all things artistic. Simon Fleet was friends with the pre-war legends of the arts and the up-and-coming young equivalent. Through him, and with him, I met and made lifelong friends (a list so long and varied they deserve the page to themselves) all of whom— and now is the moment to use the word—*inspired* me.

Their inspiration, however, was tempered with a desire to go to America. I had been to New York with my mother a few years before, and its shiny yet somehow innocent glamour had immediately seduced me. But to make such a journey without a profession, let alone an

inkling of how to actually work? By chance, with my greatest friend, the photographer David Bailey, I went, and, by greater chance, was offered a job in the art department of American *Vogue*. Now, I imagined, magazine layout could be my career. The editor, Diana Vreeland, all of New York, and, indeed, all of America, were infinitely inspirational. Eventually, I was to live in several parts of its diverse landscape, observing, reading, and learning. In each place, almost unconsciously, I found I was doing what, at the end of a decade, I'd begun to realize was the "job" I most enjoyed: decorating. A new, fascinating journey had begun.

It meant a return to my origins. Over time, these had shifted somewhat; some old friends were no longer, many young ones had become megastars. I had to embark on what was to be my finally discovered vocation with gentle persuasion, obvious passion, and oodles of charm. The years in America gave me a head

My parents had a house in Hanover Terrace, Regent's Park. Judging by the only photograph I have of it *(below)*, the décor must have been very different from Hundridge, as it's a sort of 1920s precursor of Art Deco. Maybe another of my father's good mates, the playwright Edward Knoblock, who was a dab hand at interior decoration, helped him here. But Geoffrey Scott was certainly around, as he lived in the mews house behind, in a bedsit of supreme elegance, as John Hookham's watercolors prove *(opposite, far left, and right)*. It was in this room that Geoffrey and the author and garden creator Vita Sackville-West *(opposite, center and right)* carried out their short-lived but torrid romance. After Eton, and longing to "hit the town," I moved into our London house. A new culture was emerging after the bleak war years, and I was ready to embrace every latest fad.

start: the profusion of up-to-the-minute ideas, of inspiring architecture and design that I'd observed and retained, were quite a contrast to prevailing English taste, and the first commissions I carried out were mainly for young bucks who welcomed a sleeker environment.

As time and confidence progressed, I found myself branching out and being bolder. Invitations to legendary houses of friends, in the UK and in the rest of Europe, and visits to marvels in, say, Berlin, Prague, Vienna, Rome, and Saint Petersburg, began to give me the courage to assimilate the classical style—and to realize that, fundamentally, eighteenth-century designers and craftsmen had come up with perfect designs in almost every sphere. It was a matter of taking the example of those masters a little further, understanding there are rules—some to be subtly broken—and adapting what I'd observed of the past into a mellifluous style for the present. Four decades on, I feel deeply proud of the uniquely varied designs my team and I have created worldwide, and grateful that youthful observance bestows that sublime gift, inspiration.

GROWING UP

My father and mother had been born in 1887 and 1896 respectively, but living though two world wars and the inherent social changes had modernized them, so my childhood was old-fashioned only in the sense of my having inherited from my brothers a nanny, whom I adored. With my brothers off at school, I grew up in the adult world of my parents and became urbane sooner than most kids. I scraped into Eton, where the beaks indulged my passion for painting, and turned blind eyes to my forays to London with unsuitable companions.

After school I plunged into the vortex of a London shaking off its parochial persona and becoming dazzlingly cosmopolitan. At Simon Fleet's house, the Gothick Box in the heart of Chelsea, I met many famed figures who became generous influences on my future, while I was able to add my ascendant contemporaries to Simon's potpourri of parties.

My Haslam great-grandfather was born before the French Revolution (1787–99), and my grandfather, 70 years later. I have his love letters *(top right)* to my grandmother, shown with her children, my father William in the middle. I am the youngest of his sons and the least clever *(above)*, but managed to squeeze into Eton. Thankfully, my art tutor, Wilfrid Blunt, appreciated my meager scholastic abilities *(right)*.

COPY.

The drawing Schools, Eton College. Windsor.   July 12th 1956

Nicholas Haslam has been my pupil, for painting and drawing throughout his time at Eton.

I consider him exeptionally gifted. Unlike many boys, he is never short of ideas, and these he carries out with vigour and enthusiasm. He shows great orinality, and has already a good command of technique. It is impossible, in the limited time allowed for art here, for any boy to give as much time as is desirable to drawing; his drawing is by no means bad, but if, as I hope, he is able to settle down to serious work at an art school, attention to his drawing will be his first need.

He is the most potentially gifted boy of his generation here, and has carried off one by one the major art prizes. I have little doubt that, whatever happens, he will make painting his career, and I very much hope he will reach it by way of Corsham.

(signed) WILFRID BLUNT.

Senior Drawing Master
Eton College.

The late 1950s were innocently wild, based on Brando and a new beat *(right)*. I'd learned The Twist on holiday in Paris, where it was all the rage. Before long, David Bailey, Jean Shrimpton, and I were dancing it nightly at The Saddle Room, the first discotheque in London. The *Mirror* photographed me at the Satire Club *(below)*.

THE TWIST!

The world's WACKIEST dance comes to Britain

IT is called The Twist—the wackiest, gayest dance since the Charleston. And it looks like being Britain's latest dance craze.

Already it is catching on in London. These pictures of The Twist were taken by Mirror Cameraman ARTHUR SIDEY at the Satire Club, run by Lord Ulick Browne, where he and bandleader Paul Adam have made The Twist top dance.

Rock Beat

Here's how you do The Twist. It is danced to a rock beat—in twos, threes or even by yourself. You do not touch your partner, and hardly move your feet.

Your hips, too, keep busy or less still.
But first you move those shoulders and knees.

BEND.. Follow my studio how she does The Twist

AND TWIST.. Now they're twisted—weight to left foot.

...AND BEND He's leaning over backwards to dance the Twist—this is one of the variations.

DOUBLE BEND! He bends forward. She bends back. It's a double bend that can have the onlookers bent double with laughter. But twenty-two-year-old model Natasha and Nicky Haslam, 22, find The Twist exhilarating. They are two of the few people in Britain who know how to do it.

This was surely the most exciting and rewarding moment to be on the cusp of adulthood. On a vacation in New York with my mother, a young soldier and actor named Raymond took me to Tallulah Bankhead's. I'm holding her puppy in this photograph *(right)*. Tallulah became a great friend when I was living in America, a decade later. And I am still wearing Raymond's army dog tag from the Korean War.

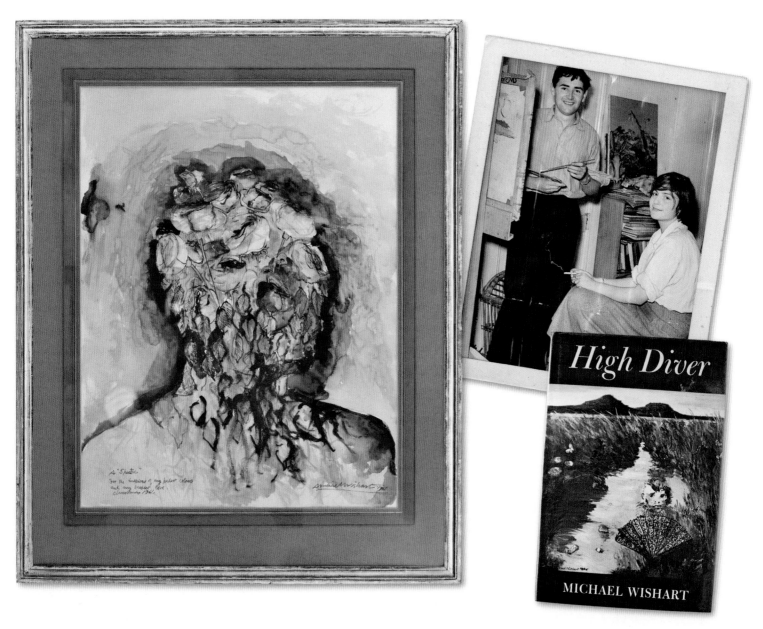

The Grand Tour

As well as the lure and lights of London, "abroad" now seemed possible, and was exerting its siren call. I had been to Paris a few times with my mother, the first as long ago as 1947, when she had wanted a companion on her quest for "New Look" clothes, and later to New York, to visit my sister Anne and her family. But now, in the late 1950s, I could travel alone.

I went by train to Capri, an island off Naples, to stay with friends, and of course fell in love with all things Italian. Then a couple of years later, in 1959, I drove to St Tropez in the south of France, at that moment practically the most talked-about place on earth. There I met a captivating young English artist, Michael Wishart, and

I'd deeply admired a painting by Michael Wishart (*top*, with his wife Anne Dunn) at a gallery in Cork Street, London. During my first visit to St Tropez the following summer, 1959, I was taken to his house in Ramatuelle, where he painted my profile in roses (*above left*). Over the following months, Michael took me to the many places in Provence he specially loved, including Arles, where we met Picasso. When, much later, Michael wrote his memoirs, the cover (*above*) was the painting I had so appreciated.

over the next few years we would go together to Monte Carlo, Venice, Spain, and, frequently, Paris, mixing in rather different milieux than I had with my mother.

In London, and specifically at the famously louche club The Colony Rooms, in Soho, I met Michael's contemporaries: artists such as Lucian Freud and Francis Bacon, actors and writers, all of whom expanded my still fairly scant understanding of the arts and architecture.

These were also the passion of two of my closest friends. Christopher Gibbs, the antiques dealer and "King of Chelsea," even then, had a fount of visual stimulation to share. Together with Min Hogg, who was later to found the magazine *The World of Interiors*, we would sneak up the driveways of any beautiful houses we saw, often—via Christopher's already boundless knowledge and charm—wheedling our way inside to be stunned by proportion and plasterwork, and to scrutinize the scale of furniture. Then off we'd go on forbidden forays, wriggling under barbed wire, trampling through brambles to romantic ruins and forgotten gardens.

So part of my Grand Tour was, in a sense, a continuation of those that had been taken by young blades in the eighteenth century. Back at home, I saw the influence that their ardor for the classical style had re-created. Somehow it stayed in my subconscious, and was to prove invaluable when the profession that it seemed I might be OK at finally dawned on me.

Determined that my Grand Tour of Europe should provide more education than merely lying on beaches and sitting in nightclubs, Michael and I went to Venice, where we saw Peggy Guggenheim and her great collection. She took us by *motoscafo* to La Malcontenta, that chimerical Palladian villa hidden among shallow canals, fringed by weeping willows. I painted the watercolor *(below)* as a memento, trying to emulate Michael's ghostly landscapes, like his of the Guadalquivir estuary in Spain *(below left)*. I'd found such gentle pictures appealing ever since my father had given me the oil sketch of moonlit gates in Tuscany by Kate Kinsella *(bottom)*.

The American Dream

I know it's a cliché, but anyone who didn't experience living in New York in the early 1960s cannot imagine the sheer bliss of that city at its apogee—a mix of shiny confidence and elegant past. Much as I had loved my life and friends in London, to suddenly be part of the heady whirlpool that was Manhattan at the time was utterly magical. Even more so if one was young, male, and English, as the London I had left was, via music, art, and fashion, gradually flowing into the conscience of America, which had not yet started on the path of questioning the customs and beliefs of 300 years.

It wasn't hard to establish my creative and social credentials in this buzzing, receptive city *(below left)*. I had the most exciting and interesting job at *Vogue*, and many of my English friends—David Bailey, Cecil Beaton, Fred Ashton, the Stones, and the Beatles—visited frequently, and I'd made many new ones. I did miss my more urbane friends, Simon Fleet and Christopher Gibbs, and the more outlandish ones. Happily, the most outlandish of all, Stephen Tennant, sent an irregular stream of his idiosyncratic letters, rococo-written in green or purple ink, his flights of absurdity a hoot on every page *(below and opposite)*.

The luck of being employed by so prestigious a company as Condé Nast and working on *Vogue*, its most admired publication, meant I was able to bring English insight to the magazine and its editors, chief among them Diana Vreeland, who quickly became a beloved friend. I also made wondrous new young ones, particularly Jane Holzer, a ravishing, kooky girl with an immense mane of blonde hair, without whom no party or late night at the Peppermint Lounge discotheque was complete, and Andy Warhol, a softly spoken artist whose meteor-like ascent would change our concept of art.

There was also the old guard: Distinguished matriarchs of grand families, such as Astor, Woodward, and Whitney—the most magnificent of them all, Consuelo Balsan, formerly Vanderbilt and Duchess of Marlborough—many of whom were still traveling between mansions on Park Avenue and *hôtels particuliers* in Paris or Rome. There were tycoons like the Paleys, Babe renowned as the most beautiful woman in America, while her husband Bill ran CBS. There were legendary architects—Philip Johnson for one, who lent me his apartment—photographers Horst and Penn, writers and musicians. We went to the opera at the old Met,

Diana Vreeland was outlandish, too, and her unique viewpoint could make the utterly banal enthralling. As a boss, she was encouraging, inspiring, and a great lunch companion. When she was away in Paris for Fashion Week, with her son in Marrakech, or in the London she loved, her looping hand brought messages showing her unbridled joy at simply "being" *(top)*. She was among the first to see the genius of Andy Warhol *(above left)*, and often the last to leave Studio 54.

dined in legendary restaurants like Le Pavillon
with the couturier Mainbocher, and lunched at
the Colony with his great client, the Duchess
of Windsor. We went dancing at El Morocco
and frequented louche bars with Gore Vidal.

Hollywood and Broadway glamour was
mingled with all this, exemplified by Lena
Horne and the much-beloved Jean Howard,
who introduced me to my idol, Cole Porter.
When friends arrived from England, David
McEwen, say, Cecil Beaton, or David Bailey,
these worlds all amalgamated seamlessly
due to the spirit and grace of New Yorkers.
At that time, the city was still theirs, in the
sense that they all knew and loved its various,
idiosyncratic pockets and areas, before each
block contained, as now, exactly the same
branch of cheap furniture or fashion stores,
and the Avenues still had shops that were
unique to America and its traditions.

After a couple of years, I was made Art
Director—the youngest ever in the country, I'm
proud to say—of *Show* magazine. This gave me
the opportunity to be more daring and avant-
garde, running stories on underground movies,
using the genius photographer Diane Arbus for
an article on Mae West, putting Jane Holzer on
the cover as the all-American sex symbol. Then
followed a teaming up with Richard Avedon
for his one-off editorship of *Harper's Bazaar*;
we had sets made by all the newly famous
Pop artists for Dick's portraits of the Beatles
and all of Swinging London. For this edition,
the cover girl was Jean Shrimpton, and I found
a hologram eye that winked, a revolutionary
innovation in the magazine world.

There was a fascinating mix of "old" New York and new wave. I was proud to meet many of the great interior designers (or "decorators," as they preferred), including Billy Baldwin, in the center at this gathering *(opposite, top left)*, who sparked me with the idea of being a decorator myself. Among my contemporaries were the debutante I'm dancing with in the St Regis Hotel's roof ballroom *(opposite, top right)* and Jane Holzer, with whom I am "frugging" in some trendier nightspot *(opposite, top center)*. Jane became a dear friend, as well as one of the Warhol "superstars."

As Art Director of *Show*, I put Jane Holzer, photographed by David Bailey, on one of my first covers *(above left)*. Her biker cap, World's Fair shades, and apparent nakedness caused an outcry. I commissioned an astonishing portfolio from Diane Arbus on the old movie siren Mae West, which had the same effect. Then Richard Avedon asked me to assist him on an issue of *Harper's Bazaar*, focusing on young talent. The Jean Shrimpton cover *(opposite, below)* is now iconic. Dick shot my Beatle-booted foot for the contributor's page *(left)*, as I'd said I didn't have time for a full portrait. Stupid boy!

DESERT SONG

But even nirvana can pall. I gradually began to feel impelled to explore the huge, varied continent—the far West, beyond the Rockies, the Pacific coast—in search of a less sophisticated lifestyle. At length, with Jimmy Davison, with whom I had shared the unparalleled pleasures of New York, I bought a ranch in the desert near Phoenix, Arizona.

It was the first house I was able to decorate from top to toe, not that there was a top, but a series of low rooms skirted by a veranda, looking onto, uniquely for the desert, a fast-flowing river. We bred Arab horses and ran cattle; I conquered my childhood aversion to riding, and, of course, OD'd on all that cowboy gear. We found a young Hopi Indian, appropriately called Star, who, besides instilling me with the legends and crafts of his and other tribes, in no time turned into a brilliant chef. There were the remains of ancient pueblos on the sky-high mesas around us, and lithe Hopi braves, costumed in their feathers and fringes, would come and stamp out their ritualistic dances in

Cecil Beaton, here exercising my favorite Arabian gelding, Te-Wa *(above)*, often came to stay at the Arizona ranch as a break from working in Los Angeles. Contrary to all expectations, Cecil was not only a skilled horseman but fearless to boot, going off on long treks though the rattler-teeming desert. The ranch, with its native tribal and Mexican-Spanish decoration, was photographed for American *House and Garden (right)*—an evocative reminder of a carefree, but hardworking, cowboy life.

Part of the fun of those years living in the West was the excuse to wear all the appropriate cowboy gear *(opposite)*, though I see in the larger photograph it's biker gear, as I had just bought a Harley-Davidson "chopper." I've still got the jacket. Here I'm taking a young stallion, Riffle, that we'd bred, for an early training session. At the ranch in the Canadian Rockies, where we went for cooler summers, Athabascan squaws, sitting by the tracks at the tiny train station, sold irresistible, soft, beaded-deerskin clothing, but my grizzly-bear chaps were made by the ranch saddler.

LOVE
P.

the velvet-blue twilight. One spring, rain fell incessantly for ten days. Then, in a dawn's crystal clarity, we saw that the desert floor had become an emerald lawn. Unexpected bright flowers blossomed on every spiky cactus and gnarled primeval branch, and Star stood in the river guddling a sudden flurry of shimmering fish.

Those friends I'd made came to stay, and many from Europe, as well as a new intake of writers, Truman Capote among them, and several film stars from Los Angeles. I'd often go there, too, taking my Harley-Davidson bike in my pick-up, and eventually getting enough offers of work on films to warrant renting a minute cottage off Sunset Boulevard. But, standing on a beach one night, gazing at the celestial halo above the curve of the Pacific Ocean, I realized I'd taken this journey to its limit. Asking for one last bottle of Coors at the bar behind me, I resolved to return to the roots I'd left a decade ago.

Truman Capote, putting aside, for a few days, the pages of his blistering "novel," *Answered Prayers*, would drive over from Palm Springs. At the time, his companion, besides two huge, slobbering bulldogs, was, handily, an air-conditioning expert. Randy would tinker away on the roof while Jimmy, Truman, and I lolled by the pool *(above)*, the Capote fantasies getting ever wilder. I took this photograph of Jimmy *(left)* reading in the shadow of a church. He never looked serious for long, and catching him in this rare introspective mood made it my favorite portrait of him.

My Harley Panhead 350 was a classic model, beautifully "chopped" *(right and below)*. When I bought it, it was "silver" and dark blue. In a moment of mad extravagance, I had the chrome gilded and the paintwork changed to pearlized white. With a gang of biker friends, I'd zoom up the highway to the cool forests near the Grand Canyon, or, hot and grimy, down to a vast swimming pool in Phoenix, which had a towering artificial wave every 60 seconds. Sometimes I'd load it into the back of my pick-up and drive to Los Angeles. In fact, when I moved there, the Harley and my dog Jackson were practically the only things I took.

Returning to London after a decade in the USA, I found everything in full swing. Despite three-day weeks, London was beginning its rise to pre-eminence, the countryside still green, quite sleepy, and free from wind farms. I wrote columns for magazines *(right, top)*, danced with Fred Ashton in a haunted house in Norfolk *(right, below)*, went to the many burgeoning new hot spots with David Bailey and Patrick Lichfield *(far right, below)*, and hung out, as before, with Christopher Gibbs *(far right, top)*; photographing him the other day, forty years later, he had this exact expression. After several rented studios, I found a big apartment in Chelsea, and was able, finally, to design for myself. Knocking through two walls made a terrific space for entertaining, and some of my most successful parties were there *(opposite and overleaf)*.

Making It In Chelsea

Apart from opening my eyes to wildly diverse cultures, that decade spent in America had brought out in me a confident vigor—much needed, being now over thirty years of age, with no remunerative employment in view. I just had to take the dare and knuckle down to what I'd patchily been tinkering with: interior design.

I rented an artist's studio in Chelsea, and enlisted the help of some sparky girls, initially Victoria Warrender and then Louisa d'Abo, whose connections to glamorous *jeunesse dorée* meant that many of my early clients were rakes who couldn't get round to decorating their first apartments. Quite quickly, bigger commissions

came in, and I was able to move to a proper—if minuscule—office, where Tom Bell joined me.

Simon Fleet had sadly died, and the friends I'd had pre-America were, by now, serious forces in their chosen fields, particularly Min Hogg, who had just founded and was editing *The World of Interiors*, brilliantly furthering and enlightening the world's concept of decoration and design. An early edition of the magazine ran a feature on the rooms I had done for Bryan Ferry. Soon he married, and I helped him with the house he and Lucy lived in. Meanwhile, somewhat recklessly, I bought a large and too-expensive apartment in Chelsea, where I was able to hone my decorating skills.

"In this drawing room I first used that trick of creating paneling with slabs of MDF stuck on the wall, which I still frequently do."

"The banquettes on either side of the fire have gone with me to every succeeding place I've lived in."

The library *(above)*, leading off the entry hall, had a fantasy "Chinese" paper painted by George Oakes for Colefax and Fowler, and given to me by the original owner, a charming lady called Mrs Weathered. Having been on various walls of her several houses, the paper was quite dilapidated by the time I installed it, and became more so when I took it down when moving. I treasure those scraps of the original that we were able to salvage *(opposite, top left)*, as they are works of art in imagination and execution. Later, I had it copied by Paul Czainski for my house in the country.

The Chelsea apartment, in Drayton Gardens, had several rooms, each big enough for me to change the mood from space to space, some being very simple yet dramatic, such as the drawing room (*previous spread*). Black linen drapes, bordered in a strip of old sepia-colored toile de Jouy, balanced the *rouge* marble fire surround with its dark, eighteenth-century portrait bust, made, strangely, of wax. Sepia engravings kept the walls spacious and light.

The central entry hall (*above*) had a window onto a light well, which I covered, and I made the room octagonal, a shape I love. The walls, "mirrored" with foil paper, were seemingly shattered near the cloud-painted ceiling, as if the room were a ruin. The reflected candlelight and silver objects and tablecloth gave the space a magical, romantic mood for intimate suppers, but it was pretty daunting in the daytime.

I wanted to re-create my father's bedroom at Hundridge *(right)*, with the Hunting Lodge depicted above my bed as the only "readable" panel amid the swirling sienna faux-marble, like the castle above the fire in his room. Fine white linen hung in front of drapes in Colefax's oak-leaf chintz — one of my all-time favorites *(far right)*. In the bathroom *(above)*, the marbleized walls around the faux-stone tub were suitably cooler. I found the hand-painted striped drapes, in front of the deep-blue shade, in a shed. The grand-looking ewer by the tub was a cheap brass number from Morocco, until I had it silver-dipped.

Home Grown

Out of the blue, something miraculous came my way. The National Trust was looking for a tenant for the Hunting Lodge, a sublimely beautiful little early eighteenth-century "folly," deep in Hampshire woodlands. After a few nail-biting months, it became mine.

The rooms in my two properties—the small ones at the Hunting Lodge and the Chelsea apartment's much bigger ones—gave me several canvases to work on in my own idiosyncratic way, unhindered by clients' briefs. It was terrific fun buying furniture and objects that only I had to like, though the finished entities (are a decorator's own spaces ever really "finished"?) were met with general approval and were photographed frequently for international publications, thus spreading the "word," and securing my company worldwide commissions.

My home in Hampshire *(opposite, above)* with thick snow icing the hedges and warm sunshine glowing on the façade. The snow makes the house look wider than it is — in reality it's the same as the distance from the topmost pinnacle to the ground. I wonder if whoever added this Jacobean façade to the original building knew these proportions.

"When I first saw the rose-pink, brick-gabled folly glinting in the evening sun, I fell in love."

Friends have given me paintings and photos of the house, and I've collected more. The photo on the left of this image *(left)* came from the Odiham Society archives and dates from the turn of the twentieth century—there's no hint of the white walls and red trim the Victorian owners decided would pretty it up, and the surrounding ancient oak forest is properly coppiced. The watercolor of the "sun" pavilion *(right)* was done by the American interior designer Mark Hampton, the day after the great storm of 1987, in which the pineapple on the roof's pinnacle was blown down. I found this oil of the Hunting Lodge by moonlight *(below)* in a Putney junk shop. Weirdly, it was painted by a relative of my friend Min Hogg.

The house's outline is like a Turkish kiosk, and the "shade" pavilion *(opposite, below)*, like its brother the "sun" pavilion, has a distinct Oriental feel. I have a theory that our Tudor and Jacobean architecture was influenced by what early travelers to the East saw. The style certainly works in less imposing and substantial buildings such as these.

By far the biggest room in the house is the garden, as can be seen in my plan of the property *(above)*. The garden is pressed into use as a dining room at every opportunity—guests shiver as yet another chicken dish is brought out. Originally, my picnics—Charles Saatchi with his back to us at the top one—were fairly Spartan, but even now, they are never as fancy as the one that was faked up for an Italian book *(right)*.

Until I made a dedicated dining room, entertaining was best done out of doors, in one of the painted pavilions, in the conservatory, or at picnics on the lawn. Sometimes now I do a big dinner in the dining room. It's fun to make the table look pretty, and I love to cook *(left)*, though dread "helpers." Many of the things I make I learned from friends in America, a welcome surprise, I hope, from roast lamb.

COUNTRY LIFE

My acquisition of the Hunting Lodge coincided with my fortieth birthday, so it seemed appropriate to celebrate both with a party. The theme was "La Chasse." People always look their best dressed for a hunt, however liberally one interprets it—and believe me, there were some wild ones. It rained nonstop the week of preparation, but the actual day, in mid-June, dawned cloudless and hot. I had put a marquee for dancing between the house and lake, over which mauve, silver, and golden fireworks cascaded at midnight. Dinner was on the lawn below the floodlit façade, accompanied by piped birdsong in the trees. With not a drop of rain to dampen lawns, fireworks, or spirits, the party went on till long after the sun rose.

Among the beloved faces here, now sadly departed, are Cecil Beaton, Nan Kempner, Bunny Roger, as a dandy huntsman, and Lady Diana Cooper, robed and laureled as her namesake goddess. Neither *Vogue* nor the *Daily Mail*, both covering it *(above)*, managed to photograph Rupert Everett, undressed as a Masai warrior, and Lady Lambton, in full rubber diving gear.

Painting the Town

The drawings I did for Bryan and Lucy Ferry's house *(opposite)*, though looking awfully wonky now, started my practice of making them for almost every project I undertake. Putting spaces onto paper as I saw them completed in my mind's eye excited clients, gave all trades involved a template of how the end product must look, and made it easier to see how scale and color relate. However amateur these early renderings, they improved with practice, and I now have a huge collection.

A great advantage of my growing career was, indeed is, being able to combine business with pleasure. Bryan Ferry (seen with me, *opposite*) has been one of my closest friends from the moment I became aware of his astonishing looks, style, and talent. The studio apartment *(above)*, which he asked me to decorate, primarily as a setting for his eclectic paintings, was in one of the first editions of *The World of Interiors*. We were both in this room when we heard that John Lennon had been shot, and Bryan decided to record "Jealous Guy" in tribute. When Bryan married, I made these sketches for the new house. Thankfully, my hand has improved somewhat since, and Bryan, as well as being a music and lyrics genius, has progressed to decorating his own homes as beautifully as any I've ever seen.

Drawing Room
at
70 Campden Hill SQ.
W8
for
Mr and Mrs
Bryan Ferry
by Nicholas Haslam

Bathroom
at
59 Campden Hill Rd
London W
by
Nicholas Haslam

for
Mr and Mrs
Bryan
Ferry

Sept
NMH
1985

Bedroom
at
59 Campden Hill Rd
London, W.

for
Mr and Mrs Bryan Ferry
by
Nicholas Haslam

The
Master Bedroom
at Epping for
R. Stewart, Esq.
by
Nicholas Haslam
September 1986

One morning, Rod Stewart (left), lithe as a panther, hair a gilded bird's nest, wandered into my office. He asked me to see his house in Essex, an amazing building—on a terrace looking over manicured grounds—in the Elizabethan Revival style. Elaborate plaster ceilings had massive stalactites, linen-fold paneling abounded, and small panes in vast windows gave onto rose gardens and box-edged lawns. Each room had a definite character. For the walls in the dining room (opposite), I had Tudor fabrics photographed onto silvered metal sheets, and the "heraldic" squares of the ceiling painted dull red and green with gilded cross-ties. The bedroom (above) was more conventional—though perhaps not for a rock star—in blues and whites and countrified chintzes.

The Dining Room at Epping for R Stewart Esqr by Nicholas Haslam July 1986

Rheinsberg, Schloß, Mus...

At the time when I was invited to decorate the salon of a mansion in Norfolk *(far right)*, I was going quite frequently to Russia, where I'd seen the mid-eighteenth-century Chinese Palace at Oranienbaum. It has the most extraordinary room, with walls covered in elaborate beadwork. Obsessed, I longed to re-create it, and here at Gunton Park, I hung panels of "beadwork," simulated in paint *(right)*, against loosely marbleized terracotta walls and a plum-colored dado. To gild the lily, I and Jena Quinn, who deftly oversaw the installation, decided to add medallions and lozenges of white plasterwork in gilt frames, adorned with "knots" of oyster shells, such as I'd loved at Sanssouci, Frederick the Great's pavilion at Potsdam *(top)*.

Nicholas Haslam 2000

Gunton Park, Norfolk

Nicholas Haslam

I was lucky enough to find the cream of craftsmen to work on my projects, from genius drapery makers, like Geoff Kent, to specialist painters, such as the Czainskis, who knew instinctively how to make the envisioned result "sing." No easy task, as I pride myself on never having a "recipe," striving to make every room unique, stimulating, comfortable, and appropriate, and always adding an ephemeral fillip that ensures people smile upon entering.

Having found so many experts to enable me to carry out the most imaginative of schemes, it was fascinating to travel to previously unvisited places in Europe. There I discovered the breathtaking gamut of decorative schemes achieved during the previous three centuries: the astonishing beadwork room in the Chinese Palace outside St Petersburg, the lipstick-pink and dead-white plaster staircase at the nearby Pavlovsk Palace, the perspective-fooling scale of the hall in Frederick the Great's Sanssouci Palace at Potsdam, the Adolf Loos bar in Vienna. Everywhere I picked up ideas, details, finishes, and colors that could be reinterpreted for contemporary interiors without looking pastiche or corny. And gradually I learned more about architecture, which was a boon when later I became involved in the design of exteriors as well as what lay behind those façades.

These three pieces of furniture *(right)* are among the collection I recently put together for OKA, Annabel Astor's brilliantly conceived stores for all things to add character and originality to one's home. The "Gothick" theme slotted in perfectly with Annabel's sure eye for classical and contemporary furnishings.

With its sky-high ceilings and lancet windows, this room, in a converted Gothic Revival chapel in Hampstead *(opposite)*, simply "sang" light, air, and pale hues. To avoid the confusion of a different curtain height for the window on the left-hand wall, I masked it as a Gothick bookcase. Shades of primrose-yellow glowed in the seating area, while the dining banquette receded with shadowy grays and dusty pink printed linen. Working on this project intensified my love of "Gothick" as a decorative style for rooms and furniture. It has a lighthearted brio, whether done full-on or with just the odd touch, which will enliven any room. With it being the obvious style for my country house, I have for years had my eye out for examples of it—the odder the better—and I use many of them as inspiration for my furniture designs. I found the original fringe-painted faux-bamboo tripod table (my OKA design is on the *right*) relatively recently, and couldn't believe it hadn't been snapped up. On the other hand, the chair on which the design below is based is one of a pair I've had since I was about twenty, and they've followed me to New York and Arizona and back. Oddly enough, they came from a long-gone shop in Pimlico, almost next to where I bought the table, which shows that a style can remain sought-after, by dealers and buyers alike, for fifty years.

MEN
IN VOGUE

The self-respect of style

From Regency to Savile Row, via winkle-pickers and cowboy chaps, NICHOLAS HASLAM, interior decorator to Rod Stewart, St James's Palace and more, reflects on style.

One of the extraordinarily lucky things about being a man is how little men's clothes ever seem to change, for centuries at a time. One only has to look at photographs taken 100 years ago and basically the suits and ties and collars are the same as now, in pretty well the same stuff.

My own theory is that the single greatest contribution to twentieth-century fashion is the comparatively recent cult of healthy good hair. Beau Nash said that any man looked smart if his shirt was clean: now the same could be said of hair. Although there ... an innovations and ... that (punk, ...

"Dressing well . . . rather li[ke] ... [in]terior decoration, has ... of perman[ence] ...

I try to [...] and deco[...] but I'm n[...] specialized[...] Nicholas [...] whose fierce[...] clients pro[...] sensitivity t[...] and a "colo[...] all his own.

le décorateur
NICKY HASLAM

Il fut un temps où Nicky Haslam était un adepte fer[...] [Amé]rican Beautifull Design. Aujourd'hui [...] d'une alliance audacieuse ent[...] le style campagnard [...] La bout[...]

Emma Soames commissioned the article on "style" for British *Vogue (top left)*. It was my first serious piece, rather than drivel about the dotty doings of my friends in *Ritz*, or restaurant reviews. The French magazine shot is delightfully informal *(above)*, but I have no recollection of what I was doing among all those stuffed birds *(right)*. Did I go bananas and buy an aviary?

MAKING NEWS

Suddenly, cameras became not only cheap, but also small. Everyone took them to private houses—unthinkable in previous decades—and guests loved it, while hosts didn't mind. Two Davids, Litchfield and Bailey, started *Ritz Newspaper*, their version of Andy Warhol's *Interview*, and in a trice its party pages ousted turgid *Tatler*-esque two-by-twos of staid Society. The paparazzi weren't far behind, in their sights the high-born hell-raisers, embryonic stars, and punk princelings; the published pictures brought fresh vivacity to papers and magazines, which in turn led to interest in what we were all actually doing. Soon, more serious articles on style-setters and interior design began appearing. With Min Hogg's founding of *The World of Interiors*, focus was distinctly on the latter.

Tricia Guild and I had terrific fun when shooting this cover for *House & Garden* magazine *(below right)*. Being the pro that Tricia is, the whole shoot was over far too quickly. I could have whispered sweet nothings for hours. *Vogue*'s Judy Britain masterminded the photograph of me for her pages *(below left)*. "Now, Lamb Chop," as she always called me, "I want you to look smart." I did my best, but what I most remember, and see again here, is how accurately the photographer captured the "air" color of the walls in my office.

HE made an assured debut as a crooner before friends only last year at a Mayfair restaurant, but now man-about-town Nicky Haslam is returning to the stage next week to perform an altogether tougher encore — at the newly renovated Savoy Hotel's art deco Beaufort bar. Accompanied by pianist and former Radio 3 host Paul Guinery, interior designer Haslam will sing his favourite Cole Porter numbers. 'It's a hot ticket,' trills a friend. 'Kate Moss has got her hands on two.'

Nicky Haslam and Emanuele Filiberto of Savoy attend the opening of The Beaufort Bar hosted by Nicky Haslam at The Savoy Hotel on November 24, 2010 in London.

Ganz schön direkt: Scarlett mit dem britischen Designer Nicky Haslam

I can't avoid name-dropping for this ragbag of press pictures, but should preface them by saying that if the "names" weren't in them, I wouldn't be, either. The top row is a goody-bag *Tatler* gave out, and below that Mercedes Bass, Kate Moss, and Emanuele Filiberto, Prince of Venice. Below them are Andy Warhol and Sophia Loren, in case you didn't know.

From the "stylish" to the ridiculous. What was I thinking, with that raven's wing hair? Elvis, I suppose. And all the punky clothing? Horrors, now, but fun at the time. There are many photos of me and beloved Cilla Black *(right)*. This is about the most printable of them. Paris Hilton and Sarah York *(below, far right)* are propping me up, with good reason, I can tell, at one of my parties. *Vanity Fair*'s legendary photographer Jonathan Becker caught me cavorting among evening shadows in the garden at the Hunting Lodge *(below right)*, while the photograph of me by Juergen Teller, taken in the sitting room there *(below, second from top)*, is more restful.

Scarlett Johansson had no recall of the lollipop shot *(left and opposite)*, when I mentioned it another time we met. Below that is George Hamilton, the chicest and funniest guy alive. I dread to think what that Russian headline says. The black-and-white picture of me photographing the Beatles on their first trip to New York is one I've treasured ever since. Looking at all these photographs, one might think that the press was permanently awash with my picture. In fact, they were few and far between, and I was enormously excited and appreciative each time one appeared. Every article was a huge boost to my career, and often gave me insight as to the best way forward. They are also an interesting record of my hair color!

RSVP

L et's face it, parties are often great fun—different people, new settings—and it's best not to be standoffish about them: as Lady Diana Cooper told me, "Go—you can always leave." By going, I've met many of the most inspirational and historic figures at parties worldwide.

Giving them is a different ball game. One either enjoys it or not. I happen to love the planning—finding the right place, deciding on the décor, the theme, the unexpected surprises.

I try to keep invitations and oddments from parties I've enjoyed. And, of course, the nicest bread-and-butter letters after parties I've given. This "scribble" (above) is, in fact, a Cy Twombly, on an invitation to one of his shows. At the dinner after, someone referred to him as Si Newhouse (the head of Condé Nast). I asked Cy to write *Vogue* on the invite and sign it Cy Newhouse. As he never signed his paintings, this trifle is unique. In this article (right), I'm with Annabel Goldsmith; her beauty was catnip to glamorous men worldwide.

The givers – the extrovert Lady Melchett (left): 'A party's no good unless you gather together a few enemies.' Interior decorator Nicky Haslam (right, with Annabel Goldsmith, wife of Sir James) thinks nothing of entertaining the likes of Lady Harlech with bacon, egg and cheese

The magic of the fleeting moment — and a man who is a master of it

Who's a party boy, then?

GREAT PARTY GIVERS

Guests are flown to exotic locations, bandleaders hired for £10,000 a night, champagne and caviar served from dusk until dawn. Glenys Roberts reports on how the other half lives it up

'A t least once a fortnight a corps of caterers came down with several hundred feet of canvas and enough coloured lights to make a Christmas tree of Gatsby's enormous garden.' So begins Scott Fitzgerald's description of one of the most famous parties of them all.

It has all the trappings: 'Men and girls came and went like moths among the whisperings and the champagne and the stars . . . There was a machine in the kitchen which could squeeze two hundred oranges in half an hour . . . On buffet tables, garnished with glistening hors d'oeuvres, spiced baked hams crowded against salads of harlequin designs and pastry pigs and turkeys bewitched to dark gold . . . People were not invited – they went there.'

The party, of course, is not a great success. No one knows the host who is trying to make up with all this abundance for a lack of social graces. So what makes a great party and what makes a great party giver?

One of the very few hostesses left in London who entertains on the grand scale is Sonia Melchett, an extrovert blonde in her mid-50s in whose yellow Chelsea drawing room Anna Ford threw the famous glass of wine over Jonathan Aitken, then chief executive of TV-am. Actually, nowadays she is Sonia Sinclair, married to the Old Etonian novelist Andrew Sinclair – who's six years her junior – but after 25 years of marriage to the third

Baron Melchett, first chairman of British Steel and grandson of the founder of ICI, her guests still think of her as Lady M. In her 11 years of her as widowhood, she was known as the merry widow. 'I went on giving parties – it was the only way that I could cope,' was her attitude.

Great party givers are usually born, not made, and usually into extravagantly wealthy families – or they marry into them. No news is bad enough to make them feel antisocial, and too bad if it's the butler's night off.

Elsa Maxwell, the famous Hollywood hostess, was once sharing a house in Beverly Hills with the man who owned the Hope Diamond, but they still couldn't attract staff. Elsa minimised her work by issuing everyone with paper plates and

126   OPTIONS · DECEMBER 1985

Regine and Nicholas Haslam
request the pleasure
of your company
for
Andy Warhol
on Thursday February 7th

R.S.V.P
Nicholas Haslam
736 6083

Cocktails 6.30–9.00
Regine's, 99 Kensington High Street
London W8

Regine's, for thirty years queen of nightclubs in Paris and Monte Carlo, opened a club in London, on the roof garden of the old Biba store on Kensington High Street. The first big party was one we co-hosted for the Warhol gang *(above)*. It's hard to believe people answered invitations merely by telephone in those days—but probably far simpler.

Paris Hilton sent me this "thank you" collage *(above)* the day after my last big bash. The only other person out of several hundred guests to send something handmade was Tracey Emin. I am at a dinner at the Cannes Film Festival with the very young model Lily James *(left)*, who doesn't look a bit pleased at having to pose with an elderly man.

VANITY FAIR LETTERMEN

Nicholas Haslam February '90

I am also one of those people who thrives on the seat-of-the-pants adrenaline that all must be perfect, for a few hours, for one night. By giving my own parties, and designing them for other people, I've learned much sleight of hand, besides realizing that less is not more: opulence, fake or real, is key. Diana Cooper once told me that the real secret to a good party is "too much to drink and a chocolate pudding."

When Tina Brown was editor of *Vanity Fair*, she asked me to design parties for her. For this one, I thought it would be fun to have guys dressed in black body stockings walking around with huge letters spelling the magazine's name, and inadvertently making other words. My drawing *(above)* shows TINA across the middle, but one can work out several others.

For some years NH Design decorated the tent at Cartier's polo lunch. The themes got wilder each time. The last one was a mad mix of swan's-down chandeliers and fake-lobster table centerpieces *(opposite, top)*. I made this cardboard cutout of Oscar *(opposite, below)* to thank Graydon Carter for many years of inviting me to his renowned *Vanity Fair* Oscar night dinners.

I'd been asked to find a stunning venue and design a birthday ball given by Laura Weinstock. Luckily, Forbes House in Belgravia, the site of the Diaghilev exhibition that had bowled me over in the 1950s *(right)*, was available. That staircase was my instant inspiration, as it had been Richard Buckle's, the exhibition's organizer. Guests were greeted by a waterfall flowing down the stairs from a fountain—in fact, lights playing on bubble wrap *(below)*.

As dinner was announced, the "water" was whipped away, and fifty guardsmen in Ruritanian uniforms lit the way upstairs with flaming torches, past windows swathed in "crystal" folds (also bubble wrap) *(opposite)*. I suppose in my mind were those MGM musicals camped up by Busby Berkeley, or the more stylish ones designed by Tony Duquette *(left)*. At Tony's dinners in a Hollywood movie studio, which he had converted into a fantasy pavilion, I met such legendary characters as Zsa-Zsa Gabor, Doris Duke, and Clare Boothe Luce.

A couple of times I was asked to decorate the Royal Box at the ballet. It's no easy task. You get given about two hours flat, and during that time the detectives and sniffer dogs come and all work stops. I am talking *(left)* to Queen Elizabeth The Queen Mother at the reception following one of them. I cannot think what I was telling The Queen herself at the Royal Academy *(below)*. She looks appropriately mystified.

Black tie
Fancy Dress

Barbara Windsor had told me she'd never met Prince Charles. Bravely, I presented her *(right)*: "Miss Windsor, meet Mr Windsor." I am so happy that some invitations, in recent times, haven't been lettered in formal copperplate, as many now are works of art in themselves. I've kept the one below, as it's not only beautiful as a painting, but so lively and joyous in its colors and haphazard informality as well. It's also conducive to supporting the important cause for which it was given—and which afflicted Roz Shand, the mother of the two hostesses— the National Osteoporosis Society.

Camilla Parker Bowles
and
Annabel Elliot

invite you to join them

for an evening of enchantment, fascination and the unexpected to be held at

Saturday 13th September 1997

7.30 pm – 11.00 pm

to benefit the National Osteoporosis Society

Talisman, Gillingham, Dorset

Tickets £100 per person

I designed this supremely ephemeral arch *(far left)* to lead into the ballroom for a party at the Savoy Hotel. The colors and style of the dress Joan Collins—who is anything but ephemeral—is wearing *(left)* might have been my inspiration, but in fact that photograph was taken some years before, in Hollywood, on the set of *Dynasty*. Not long after, I accompanied Princess Michael of Kent to a London first night *(below)*.

The queen and Jeremy Tree, her horse trainer, were sitting just in front of me the only time I've been to the Badminton Horse Trials (*right*), and were rather more interesting to observe than the dressage. I'm not much good at drawing faces, but these two sketches (*far right*) look fairly like the subjects, so for once I didn't throw them out in sheer embarrassment.

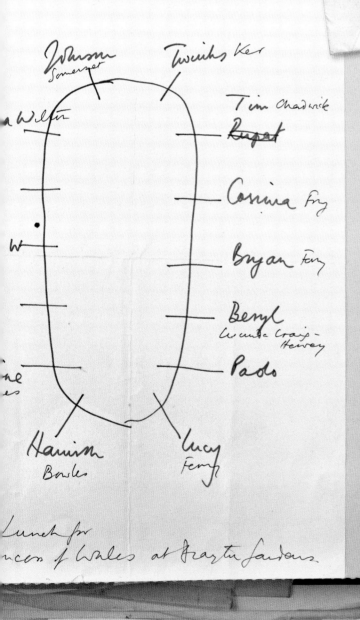

Princess Diana came to lunch at Drayton Gardens, and I asked a mixed bag of friends to join her (the seating plan is shown, *left*). I've forgotten most of the menu, but I do remember that the dessert was Sticky Toffee Pudding, as Diana had asked for it specifically—and wolfed it. Afterward, she sent me a dead-chic tie from Hermès, which I often still wear.

Diana Vreeland's lacquer-red initials *(bottom left)* are almost as vivid as Jane Russell's lips *(below)*. We met at a party in Los Angeles and I nearly swooned, as she has been a pin-up of mine ever since *Gentlemen Prefer Blondes* in 1953. In her eighties and still fearfully glamorous, she was fascinating about Hollywood when it was still a town dedicated to movies rather than television. Anthony and Carole Bamford took the new style for invitations to its apogee in this marvelously designed and lettered masterpiece *(below right)*. It was done by Alec Cobbe, who, besides being a consummate artist and living in ravishingly decorated houses, is a brilliant musician with a huge collection of pianos, Marie Antoinette's among them. The clutch of more sober invitations to a variety of events *(opposite)* speaks for itself and holds volumes of memories for me.

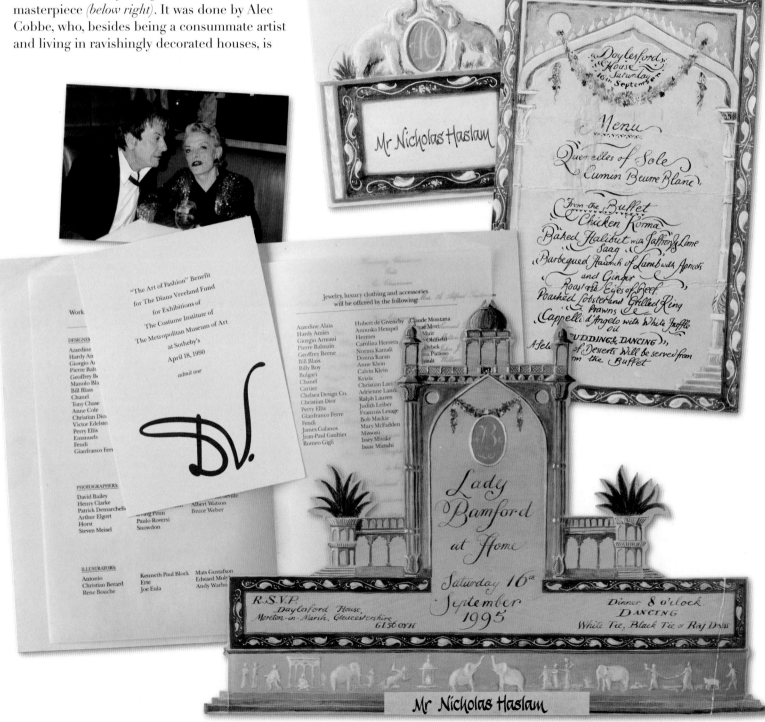

My initial sketch *(left)* for the entrance hall at Decorex International turned out to anticipate pretty accurately the actual thing when all the props were assembled *(opposite)*. The astonishing silver shell bed set the theme for a romantic, slightly surreal "grotto" bedroom. Ghostly plaster statues, with branches sprayed white, towered against the sky-blue niches and were echoed in the vast white cobwebby chandelier. Curved balustrades of purple-patterned Dutch tiles surrounded a floor made entirely of shells—it had to be a floor people couldn't walk on. Dramatic lighting was essential, as the ambience had to seem like nighttime in broad daylight. We were about to add a new design to the "Random Harvest" collection of NH fabrics, conveniently called "Grotto," so we used the early strikes of it on the walls; the final version is the border for these pages.

Dear Nicky,   October '11
How wonderful to see you at Decorex. You look fantastic! I only wish I had more time with you as you remain a terrific inspiration and are truly the best designer in the world. Next time I'm in London let's have tea. Warmest regards,
Barbara Barry

ALL THE WORLD'S A STAGE

SO IT'S SAID. BUT IT'S ALL TOO RARE THAT I GET THE OPPORTUNITY TO DESIGN SOMETHING THAT PEOPLE CAN ONLY GAWK AT FROM A DISTANCE, AND NOT WALK AROUND IN IT AND MUCK IT UP. THIS DÉCOR, WHICH I DID A FEW YEARS AGO FOR THE ENTRANCE HALL OF THE DESIGN TRADE FAIR DECOREX INTERNATIONAL, EXEMPLIFIES IT PERFECTLY.

We started the design process by seeing what bits we had knocking about in the studio—stuffed into cupboards, say, or in storage. Then I did the drawing *(above)*, incorporating them. I'd had the larger-than-life papier-mâché statues and the enormous chandelier of cobwebs and pearls made for a party I'd given a few years before. We found some boxes of shells in God-knows-where, and knew how to get more, to create the wonderfully unwalkable floor. Then Wayne Clarke produced the incredible silvered shell bed. The result seemed almost comparable to that magical Diaghilev exhibition that had thrilled me, so long ago.

Barbara Barry, the American interior designer, whom I greatly admire, sent the most appreciative letter after she visited Decorex *(above)*. I am sure this grotto is not to everyone's taste, but if a *copain* with such a pure eye as Barbara approved, I'm happy.

"It's far more intense creating something ephemeral than doing 'real' interiors."

ELEMENTS of DESIGN

I have a theory, unproven but possible, that all "design" evolves, over time, from earlier periods. The shape of early paneling is roughly that of animal hides, which blocked drafts when hung on the log walls of primitive huts. Later, milled wood meant panels could be large, gradually being embellished with baroque and rococo carving. Similarly, bits of wool stuffed into chinks evolved into woven, painted cloths, then tapestries. Dirt floors got wet, then dried hard, and *voilà*: tiles. Rooms got bigger, taller, and needed more light than that provided by tallow or wax candles. Anything reflective helped; simple glass became mirror, and the edges of panels were made silver (which tarnished, so gold replaced it). With the invention of whitewash, walls became pale; stories added above had wood floors, and the tapestries on them became carpets. With each progression, design became more intricate, plaster embellished cornices and ceilings, and fires were given stone or marble surrounds. This remained the norm until the arrival of electricity, when spaces gradually turned into sterile boxes with stark lighting, which we now call minimalism.

Statements and Gestures

I am a firm believer that bold gestures, be they in shape, texture, or color, are a requisite of good design. They somehow draw together all the things that will eventually create the completed room. It's good to plan such statements from the start, not add them haphazardly at a later date. I like to make the most of any given element in a space—increase the importance of a fireplace, add surrounds to doorways, and pay special attention to ceilings, which always look better treated with anything but a slosh of white paint. A great designer friend, Tom Parr, once told me, "Pay attention to your corners." It's very good advice. So often they end up as dark, unloved waste ground, but if curved, so the room reads oval, or with receding tiers of rounded shelves built into them, corners become both integral and useful.

FAUX ARCHITECTURE

Of course, any style of décor, even minimalist, can be given oomph by introducing architectural elements to provide a sense of scale. For instance, a couple of tall, column-like structures—narrow bookcases, perhaps—reaching near the ceiling, on opposite walls, add a rhythm by creating separate "compartments" that can be treated with subtle differences within the whole design. Even in comparatively small spaces, overscaling "fake" constructions like that, and furniture too, makes the room seem bigger and gives a sense of surprise.

When it comes to cornices, if ceilings aren't very high, it's often better to have no cornice, or to put a false one flat on the ceiling, which takes the eye "up and over" the surface. Tall walls should have the strongest possible cornice, preferably plaster—nothing's worse

This Manhattan apartment, right up under the sky and overlooking a toy-town Central Park, immediately told me, with the inner voice I believe many spaces have, what it needed. "PLEASE," it whispered, "put some curves into this series of big, bland, barren boxes." It didn't add "boring," as the building. layout and basic structure, let alone the vistas from Long Island Sound to Liberty's torch and crown, are pretty all right. To make the rooms appear taller and more exciting, free-form, double, almost futuristic cornices have been installed below existing ceilings. The corners of the sitting room are rounded with metal-incised wood-graining. A single constructional column is clad with Doric flutes and given a balancing twin, which opens to reveal a bar. Shiny floors reflect the sky and nighttime lights.

"Curves in contemporary spaces need to be big and bold. They can be downplayed later with the installation of wall coverings and furniture."

than those mingy strips of wood. The point of such sham architectural elements is to make the mind subconsciously read the limits of the space. And with so many new reflective surfaces now available, the space can be expanded far more subtly than by mere mirror.

The ceiling, too frequently ignored, is an important element in any room. Even the simplest is vastly improved when something breaks up the surface and makes it alive with light and shadow. When there is neither space nor budget to introduce plasterwork, I love to use glossy paint—not too white and certainly darker than the cornice. Often I paint ceilings a shiny blue-gray, either right up to the cornice (which may be flat on the ceiling), or in an architectural shape a foot or two away from it. You sort of notice it but don't, which is key.

Symmetrically placed furniture, the swirling ceiling, and Doric columns frame the view from the 73rd floor *(left)*. Glowing in autumn sunlight, the Upper East Side seems as miniature as an architect's model city—in fact, an architectural model of the owner's London house sits on a table out of shot.

OFF THE SCALE

I am always astonished at the huge scale of interior decorative elements that was used in buildings in the past. And not just in monumental or public structures. We tend to think, nowadays, that decoration has to relate to human scale, but it's far more exciting to beef it up, making doorways as tall and tough as possible, for instance, and choosing interesting doors, not dreary wood-veneer panels. Fireplaces always look ten times better for being as wide as the wall allows—just stick a bold molding around them. Unless they're antique, I tend to avoid mantel shelves, which merely collect a clichéd series of "ornaments." Strong baseboards and cornices add impact. The "weight" of both can be compensated for by putting the chair rail, if there's space for one, a bit lower than usual.

The scale of what goes on the walls matters enormously. Contrary to popular belief, really small spaces look better left simply painted or plastered, or treated with big-scale wallpaper that will add gentle substance and enhance the pictures that will inevitably be added.

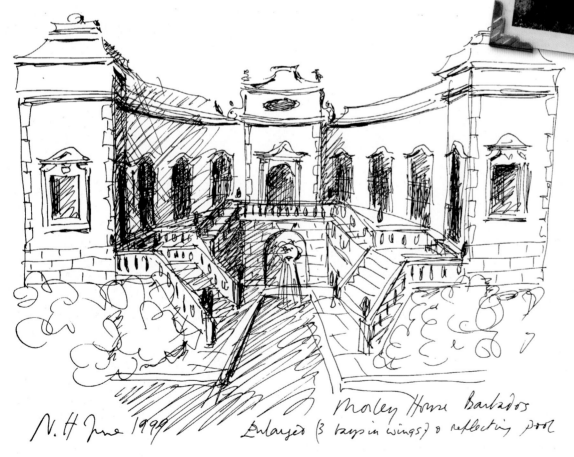

N.H June 1999

Morley House Barbados
Enlarged (3 bays in wings) & reflecting pool

Classical buildings, such as my ancestors' "villa" in Roehampton *(top)*, have always inspired me. The sheer guts of their architectural scale were an objective when designing the hall for a new-build house near Henley *(opposite)*, though the chimneypiece's brackets are tiddlers compared to the brackets at this Roman ruin in Turkey *(above)*. I have a passion for Portuguese and Sicilian baroque, and I'm endlessly sketching dream houses in this style *(left)*. The following four pages are my homage to Dorothy Draper, the American decorator, who perfected it in the mid-twentieth century.

Too often, very small spaces are dismissed with barely a thought. It was a challenge to make this minute, round vestibule *(opposite)*, part of the house on the preceding spread, have equal strength and interest. Emphasizing the two curved doorways with overscale "tennis ball" moldings, and a strong circular design in the Corian floor, defined the area; a flattened dome, surrounded by more "tennis balls" and painted bright blue, gave it a sense of height *(right)*. A carved-wood crown from a funfair ride, hung upside down as a light source, was a wacky alternative to the fairly obvious chandelier I had originally planned. The door-pulls within big concentric circles continue the theme seen on other doors throughout.

for NELLEE HOOPER from
Nicky Haslam
2006.

The circular hall at
50a Eaton Square London

The hidden door to a bedroom shown in my original sketch *(left)* is echoed by a tall, narrow niche *(above)*. It cried out for a Brancusi sculpture. Dream on. I had this version made of lacquered papier-mâché. It makes a dramatic statement, dully reflected in the strong, dark coffee-colored walls around it.

MAKING AN ENTRANCE

Halls set the "tone" of the house, providing an introduction to the rooms that come after. They should therefore be calmer, with strong elements of interest, whether that's the biggest table that will fit, a fireplace, or a staircase. Stone floors are clearly the most practical, but wide wood boards can look wonderful—never parquet, too fiddly. If the stairs rise from the hall, ideally they should be the same material as the floor, or painted to imitate it, unifying the space. Ironwork makes the best stair rail, and painted banisters look far more inviting than plain wood ones, except in "rustic" settings such as farmhouses, log cabins, and chalets.

The large hall *(opposite)* is another view of the one seen on page 81. The original design *(above)* was closely adhered to. The architects and I worked together to create it from scratch, achieving the generous sense of scale and proportion the owners required, and incorporating many of the architectural elements found in the eighteenth-century country houses that were the inspiration. The décor, too, with custom-forged iron balustrades and red-linen gathered shades and drapes, is in keeping with the traditional style of that period— except the green-painted octagonal table, which was originally a dog pen.

There is great satisfaction in making a narrow staircase look more interesting and inviting. For this upper story in a chalet in Klosters *(below)*, I felt the "necessary" stairs, against the far wall, would look lost and mingy, so I added the balcony, with a false door at the end, to give drama. It also made sense of the higher windows, their inside shutters then painted with red chevrons, or perhaps Ws, the surname initial of my dear friend Carol, the owner *(inset)*. The stairs in this *mas* in Alpes-Maritimes *(opposite)* were re-routed when the interior was reconfigured. I found an old *forgeron* along the coast who hammered out this complex three-level stair rail on site in about three days. I'd thought it would take weeks.

"Ironwork makes the best stair rail."

ABSOLUTELY PLASTERED

Plaster is one of my favorite materials. I love its age-old recipe of lime, fine sand, and water, which, when heated, crystallizes—such a romantic word. I love watching it being mixed, the clean smell when it's applied, and the cool, chalky smoothness to the touch when it's dry. Some prefer the European habit of coloring and polishing raw plaster, but for me nothing beats it "in the white," especially when horsehair has been mixed in to give strength to casts of sculptures and busts, which I like almost more than their original marble. I use plaster for models of projects I'm designing; its 3D quality gives them an added fillip. Perhaps my devotion stems from being in a plaster cast when I had polio as a child.

As plaster is practically my favorite substance, a delight to all the senses, I almost— no, I do—prefer it used for decorative elements such as statues, busts, and urns, and have plaster versions made when I can't find existing sculptures that satisfy the projected positions. These five classical goddesses, *(opposite)*, "terracotta" models sculpted in resin, were the maquettes for their over-life-size plaster versions, which now stand in a rooftop conservatory in a European capital. These original maquettes have found a new home in the hallway of my London apartment (see page 233).

Some of the rooms I love most are just white plaster, whether it's in astonishingly complicated abundance, as in places like the White Rooms that Empress Maria Theresa added to Prague Castle in the Hradčany district, or immaculately simple, such as the architect Mike Spink's interiors. Plaster makes the most beguiling maquettes, especially for staircases. One can mentally shrink oneself and imagine being inside them. On these pages is a selection of models made for penthouses both in London and Moscow. This exquisitely pure construction by Alfred Munkenbeck (*opposite, below*) is of a project for which he was the architect.

Scrubbed-wood pediments, added to the simple doorways in this house in Barbados, frame the vistas beyond *(above)*. Trellis on the walls, cornice, and architrave makes a calm but tactile surround to traditional louvered doors in a New Orleans courtyard *(above right)*. A white stone arch against deep-colored walls lifts a corridor to enticing brightness *(far right)*.

DOORS OF PERCEPTION

Doors and doorways are frequently treated as the poor relations in a room, but in the past they were often major statements in their own right, both architecturally and pictorially. I like to balance a real one, when possible, with its faux twin, perhaps chopping a bit out of the wall behind to get some extra storage—for glassware in a dining room or a hi-fi elsewhere, say. A good, strong doorcase adds brio, even if it is only various widths of beading. Obviously, anything put above a door will give height, such as the gutsy baroque motifs I've adapted *(below)*, which we had made of MDF and specialist-painted in 3D.

On the other hand, doors in contemporary buildings don't need overemphasis and are best kept as tall and simple as possible. What they are made of—rare wood veneers, bronze, glass—will speak for itself. Trelliswork around or on doors gives the illusion of infinite space, and is welcoming in its lighthearted, pastoral simplicity.

I flagrantly copied the child-like painted door paneling from the 1930s by Christian Bérard *(opposite, below left)* for the sitting room in my current London home, shown on pages 102–3. My room has a classical, deeply carved plaster cornice and ceiling, and the mix of real and faux gives a pleasingly nonchalant tension. I've also copied *(left)* these triumphantly baroque doorcases and pediments *(below)*. They give meaning, in both senses, to "over the top."

"Decorative architectural pediments and doorcases make dashingly original doorways with a sense of presence. They give the room added interest and enhance the vistas beyond."

the house. Brian Fothergill, the writer, was billeted there in April 1945 for intelligence corps training, before being posted to the Japanese theatre of war. He found himself in

There is very little here to write about – life is reduced to routine and each day is the same as the last. However, it is nice living in this delightful park – even if we do sleep

Painterly Palettes

When planning a color scheme for a room, it's essential to spend time in it at different times of the day to see the amount of light it gets, how the light falls, where there are shadows, and whether there are any murky areas that will need extra thought. After that, it's a question of deciding whether the room needs to be basically pale and seen all at once, or whether it can be dramatically darker, with pools of natural or artificial light. Then the style: trad or contemporary? (I like to mix a bit of one into the other.) Next comes an initial color-scheme decision, followed by chucking lots of different but related surfaces, paint samples, and materials onto a table and pushing them about until they sing. Now things can be eliminated and others added, such as accent colors and trims that make the rest pop. Next, decide on shapes and sizes of upholstered furniture; whether hard furniture, woodwork, or walls need painting, gilding, or silvering (or, best of all, a mix, known as gilvering); whether to have patterned or plain fabrics, and in what textures. The final choices are mounted on a board, the template for the finished room.

Trying various different blocks of color on old photographs or drawings, as Colette van den Thillart often does at NH Design, is an amusing and instructive method for getting an idea of what their effect will be in a worked-up scheme.

"Shades of white are supremely calming."

The soft white of the painted walls and flagstone floor in this entry hall *(this page)* is dramatically punctuated by black iron wall lights and chairs covered in African flour sacking, counterpointed by the elegant frivolity of an eighteenth-century gilded-lead and marble standing fountain, the gilded-metal console table and the tough swirls of the boldly carved Italian mirror frame. In a chalet *(opposite)*, a soothing atmosphere is achieved with "slapdash" plastering, designed to look like hand-packed snow, and a sleek porcelain Austrian stove. Furs on a bench surrounding it, and candlelit niches, provide a seductive note of comforting warmth.

A PALER SHADE OF WHITE

Maybe even several pale shades of white? There's almost nothing more calming and yet luminous than several different surfaces painted the many versions of that non-color. Matte, it won't reflect anything; shiny, it gleams. In either case, shadows appear stronger, creating a natural chiaroscuro.

The marvelous thing about white is that any color can look wonderful with it. Natural-colored linens and cottons spread the room wider and wider, plain darker materials stab it vividly, and patterns and flowered prints gaily enliven it. The austere or florid outlines of antique furniture cast silhouetted reliefs on simple white walls, while metal and marble gain an added coolness, yet somehow warm the pale surface behind it. The broad, sculptural leaves of trees such as lemon, the fiddle-leaf fig (*Ficus lyrata*, not boring old *Ficus benjamina*), or *Pachira macrocarpa* somehow look more attractive against white than any other color.

White rooms always look better with pale floors, whether stone or white carpets over wide floorboards. Terracotta tiles, nice as they are, seem to throw up a strange orange-brown light. Of course, those too can be strewn with white-hued rugs, including those charming old stand-bys, flokatis, but you have to be patient about their shedding fluff, which does eventually disappear.

ood heyday she often
r the bravura boldness
 white, and dark green
olutionary ideas at the
 began to use them.
lor should be treated
 but it should never be
 to get the best of a
r room," she declared.
 must be taught to re-
e feelings of those who
ve with it. Red, for in-
 with its great vitality,
ry well be too stimulat-
 one afflicted with too
 energy. On the other
 it may act as an elixir to
y or the languid. Blue,
 is always tractable, is
theless somewhat cool by
e and needs a vivid touch
ke it genial, especially in a
 in which the sun seems
icuous by
ersence."

Syrie Maugham and Elsie Mendl
were the pioneer purveyors of
all-white and, in Lady Mendl's
case, all-beige rooms. There's
no question that these soothing
monotones are superbly suited
to houses in the sun. This house
in France *(above and opposite)*
had stifling brown and orange
wallpaper and blackened beams
when I first saw it, but bleached
colors, sculptural lines, and the
minimum of decorative objects
opened up the spaces. I'm
sitting on a Maugham-esque
bench *(inset)* in a conservatory
in the Czech Republic, where
there are miraculous palaces and
interiors that make one wonder
at human artistic inventiveness.
The painting of a Mendl-style
dining room *(left)* inspired my
design for the room opposite.

"The spare 'legginess' of an Elsie Mendl room is what I had in mind for this dining room."

My painting *(right)* depicts the loggia of an exquisite little casino, now shockingly pulled down, on the old Cunard estate in Barbados. It was built in the early twentieth century, with an ancestry that was pure Palladian—light and yet shady in high heat. I added a dining room *(opposite)* to a house along the coast, designed by Oliver Messel (see also page 240). Taking my cue from his romantic vision, we lightly washed the coral-stone walls with glaze the color of sea water. Each real shell was wired in by hand, by me, and then given a light dusting of white to make them appear as if made of plaster. The Austrian "stove" is, in fact, carved wood, and contains a bar and the hi-fi.

Loggia, The Palazzina Glitter Bay, Barbados

I'd remembered seeing a mirror-topped, sea-green rococo dining table, made, probably by Jansen, for the Duke and Duchess of Windsor *(above)*. The Duchess had impeccable taste in decoration, mostly learned from Elsie Mendl, and would surely have loved eating (very little) at this replica *(opposite)*. The bedroom *(left)* was a conscious attempt to re-create a typical country-house style in the tropics.

Here is my sitting room with the casually painted paneling inspired by Christian Bérard. Gripped with this idea of faux-ism, I thought it would be fun to take it further. The fire is switch-on coals, reminiscent of my mother's when they were "just the thing," the candles are battery-operated, the overmantel is marbleized to match the fireplace, and the "Meissen" eagles are plastic bird-scarers sprayed white. One "Swedish stove" conceals rusty Victorian pipes, and its twin is a bar and china cupboard. They are topped by plaster urns holding fake fig boughs. Glazing the oak parquet floor white increased the light by about 100 percent. The off-white voile curtains have a "gilvery" shimmer; a strip of halogen set into the floor makes them opaque at night.

My own bedroom *(above)* is a chocolaty box, so tall I had to paint the ceiling the same color to lower it. The bed, my old friend of many a year, has a black-lined white canopy soaring to a baroque-style *couronne*. The inspiration for this dramatic luxury was, oddly, a drawing by Cecil Beaton, inscribed *The Bedroom of the Maid to the Duchess of Lerma*. The metal-incised wood veneer of the walls *(opposite)* links with the curved mica panels to form a shimmering "screen," which the channeled, bitter-chocolate velvet chairs root to the even darker floor—a kind of fall forest frosted with ice.

HEAVEN ON EARTH

Here is a range of colors that owes its existence to nature. The shades of umbers, originally made from earth's minerals, are, like whites, extensive in their variety. They provide a *scuro* to white's *chiaro* as an alternative to the more somber black or gray, and are more exciting to decorate with. Brown-based rooms have the same calming quality as white rooms, and there's a massive choice of shades, materials, patterns, surfaces, and finishes, both natural and man-made.

Natural, too, are all the various woods with their beautiful graining—and the expanding range of exotic veneers. Now that these are manufactured in enormous widths, they can

"From the dark chocolates to the light buffs,
all the great brown tones—the umbers,
siennas, sands—come from nature and
give rooms an earthy vivacity."

A welter of umbers and buffs in soft textures makes this London sitting room/library (above) warm and welcoming. Even the geometric trestle table in the foreground is covered with mid-brown velvet, and thick caterpillar fringe outlines the chenille sofas, fuzzing their square edges. The black TV over the mantel is mirrored by the lampshades. The reds and violets, providing a smattering of color across the bookcases, are as visually delicious as Charbonnel et Walker's finest (right).

The walls *(below)* are bark-colored lacquer, throwing into strong relief the white, overscale door surround and NH Design balustrade console tables. These are the only touches of stark white, which come as a surprise when one turns after first entering this enveloping cocoon. The triple-fold mirror screens, hiding a bar and the hi-fi, are echoed by diaphanous gun-metal voiles at the bay windows. Slashes of black—on the doors, pillows, and the African fabric on the fauteuils *(seen opposite)*—beat a rhythm.

be used on any surface, just as paneling has been through the years. Modern veneers, however, have a smoother finish than ever, making them ideal for contemporary spaces, which are so suitable for a brown color scheme.

Having assessed the effect of light and shadow in the room, throw onto the table, along with your furniture layout and other initial design ideas, your pick of earth-toned fabrics—the myriad taupes, *café au laits*, chocolates, gingers, and rusty purples—so many of which are designed and woven with a specifically natural look and touch. In brown rooms, the converse of dark against white comes into play. White furniture, plasterwork, and paint, together with these earthy palettes, give distant anchoring and glancing sparkle. You can sling in any other color, too—though nowhere is the old saying, "Every room should have a touch of pink," more appropriate than in such an earthly heaven.

Here, in the French Quarter of New Orleans *(right)*, the wall color is neither brown nor green, but an oily bronze. It's a perfect foil for the carved wood fire surround, its shape taken from the windows in nearby St Louis Cathedral, the plaster overmantel, and the pair of giltwood mirrors, which belonged to the great couturier Jacques Fath. Electric candles in hurricane lamps, above the paneled doorways, and four metal corner chandeliers illuminate the carved garlands in the eighteenth-century French overdoors. The sofas' summer covers of playful black-and-white linen mask the fudge-color velvet beneath. The antique Danish settee *(above)* is upholstered, even more playfully, in my Venetian blind material, "Shutter Stripe."

Country Life

FARMERS, GO TO IT
AND FARM BY FORDSON

This is the edition of *Country Life (left)* — February 15, 1941 — a week before the one for which my home, Great Hundridge Manor, was photographed (see pages 14–15, 18–19, and 21). I can distinctly remember scenes like the one on the cover from my childhood there, with tractors churning up long furrows of glistening earth, distant trees, and the white dots of wheeling gulls. Maybe such a natural, indeed native, English landscape subconsciously ingrained its color scheme into my dormant design cells, until one day, chrysalis-like, it developed into rooms such as those shown here *(above and opposite)*. Although they are in a London basement, the strong, dark, earthy foreground textures fading to paler neutrals, with distant greens against airiness and splashes of white, are the same overall scheme of the scene on the magazine cover. The furniture and objects even give a close-up focus of interest in the same way as the tractor, though sadly without the jodhpur-clad land girl.

"With browns, rooms can run the gamut of style, from gemütlich to ultra-sophisticated, or even a mix of both."

THESE PAGES The most newsworthy and memorable element in the Hampshire House scheme was the use of white-plaster motifs. Draper had recently hired an art historian named Lester Grundy, a propo-

shell plaster bas-reli... On completion, it wa... whether the molding... of Victorian green a... or whether the richly...

Interior decorator Dorothy Draper *(right)* was the epitome of "town" chic, whose modern American Baroque-Revival interiors were hugely influential during her lifetime (1889–1969) and continue to inspire me to this day. Anyone who has not seen her incredible interior décor at Palácio Quitandinha, a hotel high in the jungle-covered mountains above Rio de Janeiro, should get on a plane tomorrow. Behind what looks like a vast apartment block disguised as a Swiss chalet, are immense, light-filled spaces, resplendent with monumental "baroque" plasterwork, wildly sinuous balustrades, sky-high blue ceilings and never-ending sofas covered in earthy browns, stabbed with shadowy black and the reds, brilliant pinks, and yellows of the Brazilian forests' tropical flowers and fruit.

Above her appropriately power-suited shoulder is an illustration of her fearless design for a lobby at The Carlyle, a hotel in New York *(above right)*. It is unashamedly the inspiration for this dressing room in a house in London *(opposite and above left)*.

I am sure Dorothy Draper would have approved of the flibbertigibbet closet door-pulls, made of gilded-wood tassels with a cascade of bobbles, luscious as ripe grapes *(right)*. The closet doors themselves have been faced with dun-colored linen, interspaced with strips of deep-red petersham ribbon, to tone with the bobbles.

BRIGHT AS DAY

I find yellow a difficult color to use. As paint, it takes on weird reflected hues in English light: green in summer, a lumpen gray in winter. That said, pale primrose usually works, and the deep, soft-boiled-egg shade, with enough brown in it, can look great in halls and pavilions. In southern Europe, in America, and in the tropics, this animal changes its spots, as the different quality of light loves all yellows.

For upholstery, I tend to mix a rich yellow with mid-blues and strong pinks. It's a bit coy with white, but a dash of black gives it an edgy, rather military look, or a slightly surreal feeling that reminds me of 1930s posters and book jackets.

Strong, almost burnt yellows look wonderful on the exteriors of buildings in the northern hemisphere, such as the Grand Palace at Peterhof *(above left)*, where it gives soul-satisfying warmth in climates of limited sunshine. Indoors, I find it looks best used pale, with a brownish tinge and strong, rectilinear shapes, as in this dining alcove *(left)*, or with defined, all-over patterns against it, as in the floral bedroom *(above)*. The pale yellow walls in what was formerly John Fowler's bedroom at the Hunting Lodge *(opposite)* make a mellow backdrop for a selection of paintings and prints. The bow *(above)* is in "Shutter Stripe" in Haystack Yellow from my "Random Harvest" collection.

The little Chinese Palace at Oranienbaum, outside St Petersburg *(top)*, is the place from where Empress Catherine II rode out to gather up the reins of Russia following the murder of her husband, Tsar Peter III, and became "Catherine the Great" *(above)*. The Chinese Palace contains a room made entirely of beadwork, its writhing floral designs scintillating against a glowing golden background. The drawing-room *(right)* glows in the same way, as the yellow of the walls has plenty of umber mixed in, acting as a foil for both the brighter yellows in the furnishings and the paler shades in the room beyond.

The fireplace end of the room
shown on the previous page
(opposite), with its pagoda-like
carved wood pelmets, which
were more elaborate in my
original sketch *(above)*. It is
peculiar to the UK and USA
that complicated pelmets can
be created, as most windows
in mainland Europe open into
the room and get in the way
of any swags; external louvers
are used instead of heavy fabric
inside to exclude the elements.
The yellows used here are
reminiscent of the earthy tones
in porcelain or faïence, such as
the modeled "barrel" of oyster
shells or the naïve stoup *(left)*.
Artefacts such as these give
much inspiration for color
and pattern combinations.

"I always wanted to put a fringe on these pelmets."

GREEN PASTURES

It may be "green for go," but I find it a most arresting color. There are multiple, marvelous shades of green, and their freshness or tranquility always give us a sense of clarity or coolness, both in nature and design. From the innocent greens of spring to the languid, dark leaves of late summer—what I think of as "navy-green"—all are terrific to decorate with, and always with plenty of white counterpoints. I love, too, the gray-greens of rushes and grasses, soft and silvery—in fact, actual silver often suggests itself in schemes based on these hues, whereas gilt can look a bit stark.

Another great variant is glossy green with some raw umber added, which gives a sort of bronze sheen, like oil on water. It's a seductive, glamorous color, ideal for halls and stairs. I remember it in the entrances of many apartment blocks in New York in the 1950s, with architraves and cornices painted a "broken" white—white with a dab of black and umber.

The gray-green trelliswork outside this pool house in the South of France *(opposite)* is repeated inside and complemented by the shadowy grays and ashy lavenders of the covered furniture *(top)*. A long sofa stretches below panels of gilvered faux leather, which reflect natural light in the daytime and candles at night. The lush green foliage outside the louvered windows is as verdant as the view from my bedroom window at the Hunting Lodge *(above)*. The lawn is mown crosswise in alternate directions for a checkerboard effect.

The hall of my apartment *(above left and opposite)* is papered with green bamboo wallpaper, custom-printed for NH Design. Above the green baseboard is a Mauny border that resembles white nailing. The dull-metal ceiling reflects the floor's painted "stretched cloth," strewn with Dalí-esque motifs, and intensifies the wall color, like the high-summer green seen in landscapes by Fragonard *(right and overleaf)*. A hidden door *(opposite)* leads, via a corridor, to bedrooms and bathrooms, and tall double doors outlined in scarlet petersham *(above)* open into the sitting room. Touches like the shell light underline the slightly surreal ambience. Almost every inch of our new offices *(above right)* is painted a shiny bronze-green, like oil on a pool. In sunlight it's golden, whereas cloudy days make it almost white.

"I was clearly obsessed with faux beadwork at this time."

This bedroom, in a house in a Georgian square in Dublin *(left and below right)*, was vaguely inspired by one in Italy *(right)*. Parchment-colored panels were applied to very pale green walls, with a stronger green on the closets. The "beadwork" was painted by Lizzie Porter, as were the scrolling ribbons that imitate bell pulls on either flank of the marble fireplace. Wacky, 1930s painted tin lamps with tole shades stand on the triple-tier tables beside the bed.

Initial Concept for an Azulejos Banquet
in the new Breakfast Room at 120 Eaton
for Mr and Mrs M.... Nooo   , by
Nicholas Haslam 1994

"I recently went to a wedding in Portugal, and the interior
of the tiny white church was nothing but azulejos—walls,
ceiling, the lot. It really was a blue heaven."

Scheme for the Pavilion at 13 T... W3

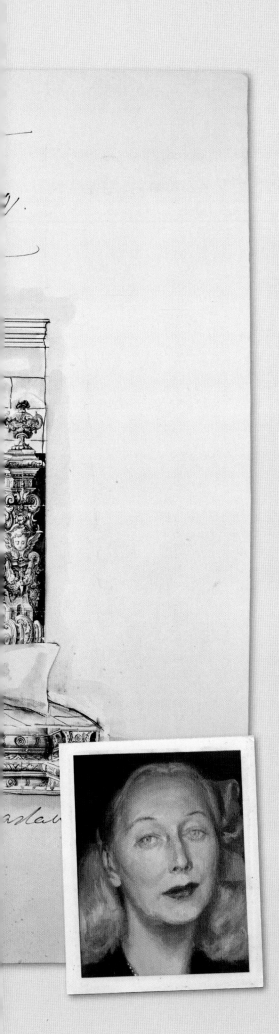

BLUE HORIZONS

Everyone has their favorite shade of blue, but I can't decide—I simply love 'em all. But it really depends on the room in which they are used. I've always avoided blue dining rooms, unless they are very pale and lighthearted or semi-outdoors. Darker shades of blue in more enclosed spaces just don't seem compatible with food and fun. Apart from that, your world is a blue heaven.

Obviously, blue is a restful color, but it can also be stimulating in its most vivid hue or sink into the background if the tone is grayer. Shades of grayish blue, like a dull sky, are a good choice for outdoor woodwork—shutters, for instance, or furniture. I also like to paint ironwork a very, very, very dark blue, as it typically was in the eighteenth century.

The dominant color of my childhood memory is blue, from the china-blue of my mother's eyes *(left)* to the faded blue of Aertex shirts *(above)* and, later, to the first blue jeans, dark and stiff, my sister Anne sent from New York. It's a hue that "works" in all its multiple shades, from the smoky gray-blue of the garden-room design *(top)*—which, I admit, I largely nicked from a magazine—to the throbbing brightness of this tiled garden seat *(opposite)*, inspired by Portuguese *azulejos*.

"The cloud-like curves of the cornice, also covered in pale blue silk velvet, echo the sky beyond."

The air-blue silk velvet covering the walls and bed, and channeled on the custom-made upholstered furniture, continues the skyscape all around the bedroom of this Manhattan apartment *(right)*. The whiteness of the wide, tall windows is balanced by simple linen sheets and the coral-branch china bedside lamps (just in shot). Matching blue shagreen forms the writing surface hovering above a Lucite NH Design desk, with its low-armed chair wrapped in bleached vellum, by Karl Springer. Darker blue lamps *(above)* with battleship-gray shades seem to float on their Lucite plinths, adding to the purposely insubstantial atmosphere of the room.

"A staggering amount of fringing was used to cover this wall."

The most astonishing room I know is the Hall of Mirrors in the Amalienburg *(below)*, a pavilion in the park at Nymphenburg Palace in Munich. The walls are a soft robin's-egg blue, festooned with a riot of silver-gilt rococo plasterwork—garlands, trophies, banners, urns, waterfalls, and branches, surrounding huge, wonky mirrors, and teeming upward, over and above the cornice, tendrils and birds silhouetted against a chalk-white ceiling— all lit by huge rock-crystal chandeliers. Phew!

For this glamorous bedroom in Moscow *(opposite)*, more than 2,000 yards of fringe were used to make soft-textured walls, which were lit by the glitter of mirror and glass in a contemporary take on the salon of the Amalienburg *(above)*. The walling of cornflower-blue roses in the bedroom, with its slightly "Chinese" door pediment *(above right)*, was clearly inspired by rooms of the same period seen in somewhat quieter German palaces.

The Notting Hill apartment of Colette van den Thillart (with me, *inset*) had pale Wedgwood-blue painted walls, and needed only that china's corresponding white to create a restful harmony. Contemporarily patterned furniture, a wood-grain design carpet in olive-green, and a few surreal "careless" touches jazz up the early Victorian architecture. I'd never done a dark blue room, but when Prue Penn gave me her portrait, by Douglas Anderson, I knew that the walls of the library end of my sitting room *(opposite)* had to be the blue of her stole; luckily I found a grasscloth paper that matched exactly. I covered the amusingly high chair backs in the color of the painting's sky, and the seats in the plum of Prue's dress. Bookcases are masked by doors covered with white-book wallpaper and trellis.

Richard Parkes Bonington (1802–28) is a painter I deeply admire. I find his oil sketch of the quay at Le Havre *(left)*, with its brown-mauve shadowed foreground and pale lavender spire, a masterpiece. Giovanni Boldini's 1908 portrait of Marchesa Luisa Casati *(below)*—whom I, as a youth, once saw in her very old age—takes one's breath away by its verve and tension, the black greyhounds writhing below her violet-flowered waist.

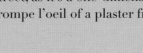

This enfilade of lilac-linen-curtained rooms *(left and overleaf)* is book-ended by bronze and sharp green in the scatter cushions and bed throw. Pale wood and stone floors and rough-hewn white beams counterbalance the delicacy of the overall scheme. The picture above the sofa, on the Mauny *papier-peint* walls, is right up my street, as it's a one-dimensional trompe l'oeil of a plaster frieze.

LILAC TIME

People used to shudder at the mention of lilac as a decorative color, even more if one said "mauve." When, thirty years ago, I did a room in mauve and green, everyone said, "You're mad," but now one sees it all over the place. It's a comparatively recent color (the chemist William Perkin invented the recipe for it in 1856) and for ages it was used almost exclusively for mourning—hence, maybe, the shuddering. But I find it magical. With half-shut eyes, one sees that so many

surfaces and shadows actually read an indefinable gray-brown-blue, which mauves or lilacs, at their most relaxed, should be.

If one studies the exquisitely thought-out flowers-and-ribbon-entwined designs in old chintzes, especially French examples, one sees that the shadows that give them their depth are, in fact, that indefinable natural color, not a ham-handed gray. This points the way to using corresponding shades—understated almond-green, mousy brown, rain-cloud blue or faded rose petal—for upholstery. Stab them with a strong color or two—a golden yellow, a bronzy green or a deep pink—and that subtle palette will morph into a glowing bouquet.

Strong lilac can also pack a terrific punch. Quite often I use it as a main color, but a mere strip of it can spark up a low-key scheme. A pencil's-width edging of lilac stuff, or lilac petersham around doorcases, gives a breath of romance in the same way as a bunch of violets nestling in the lapel of a fur coat in 1940s films.

This lilac and lime-green "Jacobite" tartan is one of the prettiest *(below right)*, and you don't have to be Scottish to wear it. The same color combination is at play in this bedroom *(right)*. The top of the antique table on the far right is, unexpectedly, made from bits of broken Roman terracotta pottery.

"*Like shadows, mauve gently recedes into the background and gives the impression of space in any room.*"

The color scheme for this elegant sitting room, in a mill house in Hampshire, is essentially lilac, but the various accent colors and patterns prevent it from looking overly sentimental.

Diana Vreeland *(inset)* famously
stated, "Pink is the navy-blue of
India," but her preference was
for bolder colors, especially red,
which, she said, "must have just
the right amount of orange in it."
Her apartment was ablaze with
vermilion chintz, patterned
with exotic Indian flowers.
It was known as "the Garden
in Hell," but I saw it as a red
heaven. The dark terracotta
of the walls *(left)* becomes deep
orange-red in electric light,
made more vibrant by the
adjacent yellow-toned fabrics.

SEEING RED

I am a signed-up member of the Red
Brigade. Red rooms are one of the joys
of the world, but they have to be pillar-
box-red, scarlet, Chanel-lipstick-red; think
Chinese lacquer. My heart sinks at the word
"claret"—too much blue in it.

Once the rarest of colors, true red—the
natural dye from the cochineal insect native to
South America—was a valued commodity, first
exported by the conquistadors in the sixteenth
century; even Corot, painting 300 years later,
could afford only a dab of it. This richest of
hues should be used boldly; its vividness
makes a small space come alive.

Andy Warhol was doing paintings of shoes *(left,*
when I first met him when I was working at *Vogue*
in New York. Later Andy gave me one of his
celebrated flower silk screens *(far left)*. When I was
feeling a bit broke, I reluctantly sold it for what
would now seem peanuts for his work. We clad the
library *opposite* in narrow lengths of zebrawood,
glazed scarlet; the background of the antique
screens with naively painted plants is the same
color I love the old Norwegian carved chair.

As can be seen from my original sketch *(above)*, I'd planned red drapes and pelmets for this little octagonal supper room *(opposite)*, which is based on the black-lacquer and faux-marble parlor in my childhood home, Great Hundridge Manor. Then I realized the room needed red-lacquer niches of the same shape on the opposite walls. The tablecloth is about as near as I get to using "claret," but it works well here for not-crying-over-spilt-wine reasons. The strong red chevron velvet on the chairs leaps up from the tapestry-like rug. In the garden room of my house in the country *(right)*, some branches of red coral found in Barcelona decades ago—I think, in reality, they are some fake substance, but who cares?— stand on the amusing tripod "Gothick" table with its painted red fringe. I've copied this quirky little table for the collection of furniture I've done for OKA (see page 55).

My first red room was in the minuscule cottage I found in the late 1950s in Waterloo, then a derelict bomb site. Christopher Gibbs lived nearby, on the attic floor of the house Wren lived in when building St Paul's, and its long, low window framed the cathedral's sooty silhouette. In this still-Dickensian part of London, my shiny red sitting room was pretty innovative. I've usually squeezed a red room into anywhere I've lived since. The "Red Room" at the Hunting Lodge (*right and above*), while not a vivid red, is filled with varied shades of it. Diana Cooper gave me the china Garibaldi (*above*), proud in his red jacket, and I collect any old red object, such as these plastic lobsters (*opposite, below*) to brighten up tabletops. The drawing (*opposite, top*) is of a friend's sitting room in Albany; it's exactly what I like, crammed with interesting items, comfortable, and yet orderly.

COATS OF MANY COLORS

OUT OF THE BLUE, BY SOME FORGOTTEN FLUKE, I FOUND MYSELF LIVING IN A WORLD OF VIVID COLOR. THIS WAS CECIL BEATON'S HOUSE IN PELHAM PLACE, SOUTH KENSINGTON, AND THE ROOMS WERE EXACTLY THE SAME AS THEY'D BEEN WHEN HE LIVED THERE.

The black velvet walls filleted in fine gilt made a dramatic backdrop for the Giacometti lamps, the Jean-Michel Frank banquettes, and the club chairs, covered with clashing purples and greens, pinks and yellows, with palest peach silk at the windows; yet nothing jarred. I say "exactly the same," but the only things missing were Cecil's wonderful pictures. Some horrors replaced them, which I immediately shrouded with lengths of lilac satin. I also added a few favorite bits of furniture that still seem to follow me everywhere.

My two years amid such vibrant surroundings taught me how to layer colors—just gulp, take the dare, no pussyfooting. The eye soon adjusted to that kaleidoscope of shades, and the shades of all the legends who had basked in Beaton's brilliant persona added another layer—of memory and laughter.

Cecil's reply *(right, top)* to my invitation to my hunt-themed party at the Hunting Lodge (see page 47) was written after his stroke. It was the last big party he was to attend. Below it is an initial doodle for my portrait by Michael Wishart (see page 26), which Cecil had so admired. I had acquired Cecil's youthful self-portrait sketch *(right, below)* years earlier. When I first brought it into this house, I swear his eyes sparkled. I seem to have taken the idea of layers of color to the extreme in my outfit shown in this Polaroid *(opposite, inset)*.

The wall finish in my dressing room *(this page)* came about accidentally. The original blue *strié* plaster had crazed, so instead of replastering, I had the cracks filled and painted with white marble veining—not a trick one could get away with in fussy people's houses, but it seems to be holding up.

Fee Fi Faux Fun

When it comes to trompe l'oeil paintwork, it's essential to seek out the best artists for such delicate work. It's also an essential tool in a designer's box of tricks. Fooling the eye with such simple devices as faux paneling must be done with scrupulous attention to the source of daylight, thus making the deception believable. Using a bit of reality, such as a painted-wood chair rail, adds to the illusion.

With many natural finishes—tortoiseshell, amber, ivory—now endangered, if not forbidden, re-creating them in paint is the only option. Likewise, as most quarries of interesting marble are either exhausted or proscribed, and what's available being pretty humdrum, faux marbling is the great alternative. People tend to be sniffy about it, but the technique has been used for centuries. Best of all, one can create marbles, agates, and all sorts of semi-precious finishes that have never actually existed.

'EAU

CHÂTEAU D'EAU

Classic faux paneling has to be done carefully, with attention paid to the various light sources to achieve the required, eye-fooling effect, such as this sixty-year-old example *(above and opposite, inset)* by George Oakes of Colefax and Fowler. Faux marble, on the other hand, can be meticulously perfect or free-form, with the sort of wild colors and veining seen in Spanish churches. The "marble" mantel surround *(left)* was based on the real marble fireplace, but looser, to blend with the cartoon-like trompe l'oeil paneling.

"Free-form faux marbling can be done with what I call an 'eyes-shut' technique."

This bathroom *(left)* is marbled to look like the real thing, as some of it actually is. Even I can't tell where reality ends and Paul Czainski's convincing technique begins. The urn is bronzed plaster.

The dining-room *(left)* was inspired by Alexander I's bedroom at Tsarskoe Selo, outside St Petersburg. After the gilded gaudiness of the Catherine Palace, the bedroom is a refuge of calm, with its cool Wedgwood coloring. I copied the general layout of bookcases and slender columns, which Paul Czainski glazed to imitate the porcelain originals. Painted cloudy skies can easily veer toward tweeness, so no fluffy white blobs. Milky-coffee colors with darker, storm-threatening edges are far more exciting and naturalistic, with sunlight and blue breaking through *(above)*.

This dark-stained, highly polished, painted mahogany lobby *(right)*, leading to, and creating a contrast with, the silvery wood-grained bedroom, has reverse-fielded door panels, bordered by gold-leaf beading. The doorcases have been decorated with a strong-veined, faux antique marble. Old books are good sources of famous collections of such amazingly bold marble seams, now mostly exhausted. On smoky blue walls in between, real white-and-gilt casts of eighteenth-century medals and seals are "hung" from painted ribbons.

Another view of the "Chinese" lacquer and yellow-marble room *(left)*, which was inspired by the sitting room in my family home (see page 17). The tone is purposely somber, but shafts of light from the windows, curtained in goffered velvet, play on the paneling, the gilt-beaded doors, and the gleaming floor, so the room is never static. At night, the same effect is achieved by reflections in mirrors.

Storks stalk, black bugs and bees buzz, and butterflies and birds flit among strange fruit and foliage in this "wallpaper" painted by Paul Czainski for my dining room in the country. It is a facsimile of the paper I was given years ago, featuring a deftly imaged fantasy landscape by George Oakes (see pages 40–1).

The bedroom on these four pages is the one glimpsed from the mahogany lobby on page 151. The silvery wood-graining was applied to the existing paneling in this Queen Anne house belonging to Natasha Kagalovsky *(inset, left)*, a St Petersburg-born American with the tenderest heart. Near unique, now, for its period, the building once stood amid Chelsea's orchards and fields, off the road (the King's Road) that Charles II made between Westminster and his country palace at Hampton Court. Tall windows have drapes of flower-splashed French chintz with a pale green background in front of *capitonné* shades of rose-pink silk. I saw the carpet late one night in a shop on Santa Monica Boulevard in West Hollywood, as I was walking, none too soberly, back from a *Vanity Fair* Oscar night party. Next morning, I couldn't remember the name of the shop or exactly where it was, but we eventually tracked down the source, and six months later the silken jewel was laid. The great photographer John Swannell came to take my portrait for his new book early one spring morning; so early, in fact, that I was still asleep (perchance dreaming?) and tousled, but John snapped me in my pajamas as I opened the door *(inset, above)*.

PERCHANCE TO DREAM

WHETHER AWAKE OR ASLEEP, I LIKE A BEDROOM TO HAVE A DREAMLIKE ATMOSPHERE, NOTHING JARRING, ALL MELLIFLUOUS. A GOOD WAY TO INDUCE SUCH A REVERIE IS BY TREATING THE WALLS WITH EITHER MATERIAL OR SPECIALIST PAINTWORK THAT IMITATES WATERED SILK; OR GO ONE STEP FURTHER—SILVER WOOD-GRAINING ON A PALE, BUT NOT TOO PALE, BACKGROUND COLOR.

In one of the first country houses I ever decorated, we glazed the drawing room a dusty pink and overpainted it with this silver wood-grain, and I'm still at it—a sort of sea-foam, gray-green being top of the pops at the moment. A simpler method of achieving a similar result is to drag a coat of chalky glaze over the base color or, better still, stretch a fine voile over the wall,

"I first did this wood-grain effect in pink for a drawing room."

The reverse-painted mirrors—*verres églomisés*—were created by that superb artist/craftsman Nominka d'Albanella. With merely a few rough guidelines on the glass, Nominka can draw elaborate freehand designs, and then magically flatten precious metals or stones into a smooth surface. For these tall closet doors *(opposite)*, she layered crystals, gold, and mother-of-pearl, to form exotic, almost liquid, flower-scapes.

gathered on rods or batons at the top and bottom. One of the most ravishing bedrooms I have ever seen was treated this way. It was in the Palazzina Cinese near Palermo, Sicily, and was created in the late eighteenth century for Maria Carolina, Queen of Naples—who, like her sister, Marie Antoinette, didn't do things by halves. So she slept, in that Oriental fantasy, surrounded by walls of sky-blue silk over which was stretched, loosely, white broderie anglaise, with a third layer of gathered white voile creating an almost cloud-like, holographic effect. It inspired me to have a go at copying it, recently, for a house in New Orleans.

"I always wanted to change the chandelier."

Curved panels of mica soften the abrupt corners of the dining room in this Manhattan apartment *(opposite)*. The metal-inlaid wood leads the eye to a canvas by Elliott Puckette, its hieroglyphic theme echoed in the creamware urn below. A long, starkly white corridor *(above left)* is terminated by double doors faced with the thinnest, crispest mirrorwork, its fragility causing a heart-in-the-mouth situation on its journey from London. The all-white furniture, lights, and objects reflected in them give an unearthly luster in close-up *(above right)*.

All That Glimmers

With the fad for so much raw glitter and glitz abounding, I find it wiser not to be pound-foolish. Although I have sometimes out-blinged bling, it must be said that even subdued, shimmering reflectiveness can cost a pretty penny.

That so many gleaming surfaces are being invented almost daily, whether by some forward-thinking industrial boffin or by young—or even old—genius artisans, determined to fuse the precious skills of past eras with the newness of now, is quite astonishing. And, having grown up with just plywood and Formica, I find it equally extraordinary that many of these cutting-edge products are not only available in almost any size and shape required, but they are also flexible, malleable, washable, and nearly indestructible. These new materials give rooms

A triple bank of corresponding mirrorwork between diamond-padded doors hides the bar and hi-fi in a London living room *(above)*, and is repeated around the bookcase wall. The carved white-wood antique figurehead complements the reflected white furniture at the far end of the space.

The bathroom *(right)* has a darker, richer sheen, with antiqued mirror panels lining the tub's alcove, and a pair of lavish rococo brackets and vases on either side of the burnished-bronze urn. The urn isn't operational, but I always try to have a seeming source for cascading bath water.

a luminosity even on the gloomiest days, and the scintillating glow of reflected lamplight exhilarates the soul as one reaches for the first martini of the evening.

There was a time—and not so long ago—when the only type of mirror available was a dull sheet of stark, staring glass. The imperfections, wonkiness, and darkened edges of old mirror-glass were frowned on. Processes such as clouding, pitting, or speckling, and, above all, the ravishing technique of *verre églomisé*, when the silvered backing is scraped away and colors or gilding are applied instead, were all but forgotten. Now all these delights are back with a wallop, shining seductively from the darkest recesses, or beaming back skylines, sunlight, and vitality from an outside world.

GILDING THE LILY

SOMETIMES I'VE SEEN AN INTERIOR, USUALLY OFF THE BEATEN TRACK, THAT HAS HAUNTED ME UNTIL I'VE DONE MY OWN VERSION OF IT. THE ROOM SHOWN HERE IS A CASE IN POINT. ITS INSPIRATION WAS AN EIGHTEENTH-CENTURY, FOLLY-LIKE TOWER, ON PFAUENINSEL, NEAR POTSDAM.

My version of the Pfaueninsel (Peacock Island) room was done for a house in the French Quarter in New Orleans, and it was an astonishingly complicated process. First of all, the genius painter Paul Czainski and his wife Janet flew out to Berlin to see the original, to which visitors are (or were) only rarely allowed. The first stage of the project in Louisiana was to put an absorbent paper on the walls, which was then gilded and afterward distressed with what smelled like a mixture of tar and oil. Once dry, the outline of the overscale, Europeanized version of a chinoiserie design, more like material than wallpaper, was sketched in charcoal so it "read" all round the room. Paul then blocked in the dark branches. The twigs and leaves, each with a reflective pigment in the paint, were next. After that, the

"This room was featured in a book titled:
'100 Most Beautiful Rooms in America'."

Pedants point out that the quotation, from Shakespeare's *King John*, is really "paint the lily," but both apply in this perfectly proportioned space. The pleasure of creating rooms for people who enjoy going above and beyond the norm is evident in so lavish a conception. Used primarily by the owners,

celebrated hoteliers Frances and Rodney Smith, for entertaining on a grand scale and in grand style, this drawing room *(above left, opposite, and overleaf)* had to have glamour and practicality. As a result, there are several seating areas and a drinks cabinet by the concealed door—handy for serving ice-cold

Sazeracs, the original New Orleans cocktail, and blackened oysters on the half-shell (don't throw away those shells, let's build a grotto). The Edwardian rococo painted-glass armoire in Frances Smith's bedroom *(above right)* initially suggested the theme for the drawing room, though set in an earlier century.

massive tree-peony flowers, glowing with ground-up mother-of-pearl. The whole room was then lacquered about three times. Talk about lily-gilding!

But there is more. Because the space is streaming with daylight from four tall windows, the glow on the walls changes constantly from silvery to deep golden. When lit by lamps and firelight in the evenings, the flowers become almost luminous, reflected in one wall that is floor-to-ceiling *verre églomisé* in the same plant-like design, but gilded behind cloudy mirror.

Creating such a room was laborious but rewarding, as it demonstrates that modern-day craftsmen can achieve equally extraordinarily inventive interiors as their eighteenth-century counterparts.

The drawing room shows its full panoply of exuberance and intimacy in the afternoon sunlight *(left and above)*. Soon, those candles will be lit, the drapes pulled, and the magic of nights in the Mississippi River Delta will flicker on the gilded-lily walls.

[1]

[2]

[8]

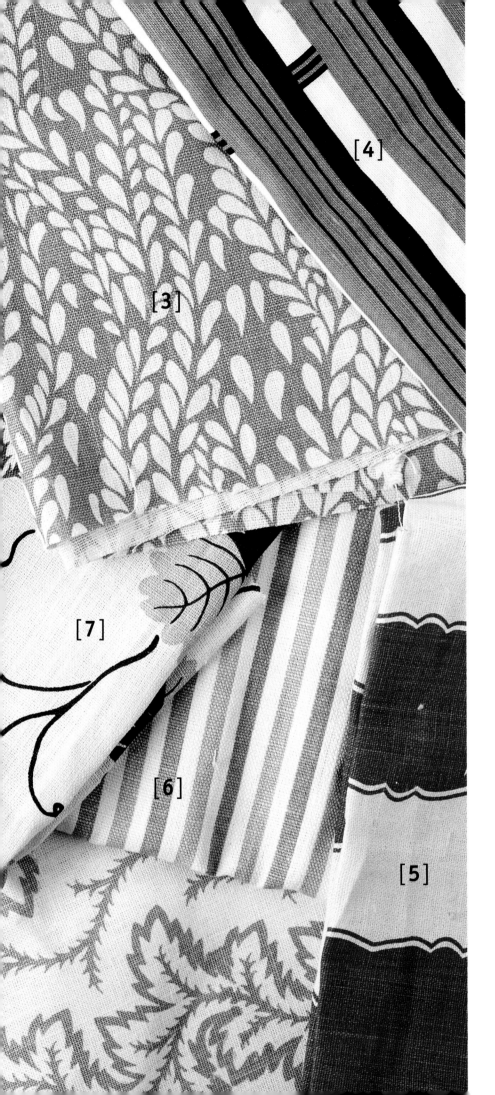

Calm and Collected

It took me quite a long time to have the nerve to do a fabric collection. When I did, it sort of happened piecemeal. I'd seen things I liked—a bit of antique porcelain, say, or a leaf, seaweed, clothing in a painting, or, that rarity, an as-yet-unplundered volume of old pattern samples—and put them in a file, so that when the time came, there was quite a lot of eliminating to do. Harder to find was the right cloth to print on. Acres and acres of beige-ish stuff was rejected, as I wanted a clean, near-white background. Choosing the colors was fun, working out repeats less so.

Having whittled the designs down, we named the collection "Random Harvest" and one of the ranges in it "After All," in honor of one of my design gurus, Elsie Mendl (née de Wolfe). It was the name she gave to her last house in Beverly Hills, and the stripes would have been right up her alley. Perversely, Elsie's favorite color was beige; on first seeing the Parthenon, she said, "Why, it's beige! MY color."

It was exciting when major fabric houses agreed to distribute the collection. One really can't ask for more than being repped by Turnell & Gigon in the UK and Claremont in America.

Here is a selection from the "Random Harvest" collection in different colorways, clockwise from top left: "Midday Lace" (1), "Seafern" (2), "Winter Wheat" (3), "Shutter Stripe" (4), "Balcony Stripe" (5), "After All" (6), "Greenbier" (7), and "Zephyr" (8).

FLORAL DANCE

Some places cry out to be given the flower-bower treatment, while others say, "Get outta here." For the former, I like to go the whole hog, preferably using the same design on everything, uniting walls, drapes, and furniture, and usually adding a correspondingly patterned carpet. Anything plain in this form of décor, especially if it's quite a big space, will look like a stifled yawn. Sometimes it's not a bad idea to use the wrong side of the fabric, particularly on walls, as this creates an echo effect of the pattern in the rest of the room, which is less frightening to the faint-hearted. This look is very embracing, imparting an instant sense of comfort. Almost any old stick of furniture gets drawn into the atmosphere of intimacy, and every picture looks far better than it probably is against its floral background.

While, perhaps, this abundant florescence is a bit hackneyed in bedrooms, chintz in bathrooms adds a wonderful whoosh of gaiety to the tedium of the daily ritual, and provides eye candy during a candlelit soak. The great secret is to avoid any stuff with a twee floral design. Go big and bold, even in the "smallest room," as nannies used to call the toilet.

The blue-and-brown-printed linen upholstery and wall covering give an overall masculinity to this small sitting room in a Hampshire country house *(right)*, as do the plain cocoa-colored cotton drapes, framed by the bookcases topped with chunky moldings. Using mainly one dominant pattern expands rather than shrinks a room, as demonstrated in an alpine dining room *(overleaf)*.

"As the immortal Nancy Lancaster observed, 'To make a room look quiet, you have to complicate everything.'"

Sprightly Lady Mendl *(left)*, in an outré setting designed by her protégé Tony Duquette; my eye is drawn to the slipper chair, slipcovered in a fern chintz, versions of which I often use for kitchens. Elsie smothered the flowered wallpapers in her Versailles home with charming pictures *(below)*; Ludwig Bemelmans's book lovingly describes her idiosyncratic whims, and a pre-war letter from Wallis Windsor goes into raptures about "Dearest Elsie's" exquisite taste in houses, objects, food, and clothes *(bottom center and left)*. My Mendl-y striped short inner curtains for windows in this Indian-chintz TV room *(opposite)* mask their lack of height.

A French material of stylized vine tendrils, grapes, and writhing garlands on walls, drapes, and a couple of chairs, plus an elaborately patterned Savonnerie carpet in classic colors *(below right)*, form the bright framework for muted greens and reds on the upholstered furniture in this Irish drawing room. The curved, chair-rail-height bookcases running all around the room were inspired by some in Pavlovsk Palace, outside St Petersburg, which is roughly contemporary with this late-Georgian house. Grape-hyacinth-colored petersham has been used to edge and "anchor" the chintz walling *(above right)*.

The idea for this bathroom in London (left) came from Le Laiterie, the dairy designed for Marie Antoinette at Château de Rambouillet. Its pure, chalky, classical whiteness seemed eminently transposable to the purpose of bathing. So did the marble counters, reconfigured in my sketch (below) as narrow tables on quiver-shaped legs. The tub surround is rare antique marble. Lantern-like cabinets are "suspended" from tin ribbons, which I love. The same chintz is used for drapes and furniture, including the seat of the antique musician's chair. For this comfortable country-house bedroom (above right), I blatantly copied my own at the Hunting Lodge, designed by John Fowler (see page 198). I had the airy design by Mauny (overleaf), the Parisian papier-peint manufacturers, custom-colored for this top-lit attic.

IN BLOOM

HERE I GO, REFUTING MY OWN "RULES."
A FLOWER-STREWN BEDROOM CAN SOMETIMES
BE BOTH REVIVING IN THE MORNING AND
CALMING AT NIGHT, WITH A GENTLE
FLORAL DESIGN SET OFF BY CASCADES
OF NEUTRALS FOR THE EYE TO REST ON.

I'm sure the trick is to use just one pattern, quite large in scale, and put it almost everywhere, with no smaller or "corresponding" versions. The quiet, all-over harmony keeps the room from being jumpy or twee. Granted, it gives a distinctly feminine atmosphere, but girls spend more time in their bedrooms than guys, so it seems only fair to pander to their sensibilities. In color combinations of brown and blue or brown and green, florals can work wonders for more masculine bedrooms too. Their occupants will be barely aware of the teeming plant-life around them, any more than they—or, indeed, I, as an amateur gardener—would be actually "aware" of the smooth and tumble of the shape of flowers, leaves, and plants in a garden. Yet these have always, clearly, inherently, and naturally, influenced the myriad colors and designs of floral schemes. Whether it's a fallen twig from a springtime oak tree, a vast overblown peony, or the spikes of a cactus, nature continually provides new inspirational motifs, forms, and contours.

The interiors shown right and overleaf are all part of the same house—a detached nineteenth-century

The glamorous young owners—he a major art dealer and she in the bloom of youthful beauty—specifically wanted the visual sensation of the luxuriant garden surrounding the Holland Park house to continue inside. In the main bedroom (right), full-blown roses ramble over the Swedish canapé and the canopied bed, while the reverse side of the same material pads the walls, giving a mistier, more distant effect. Irregularly pleated, outward-undulating pelmets over the windows mean the swagged drapes can be closed over the rose-chintz slatted radiator below. My own garden at the Hunting Lodge (inset) provides me with endless inspiration in all seasons. After years of neglect, it was laid out by John Fowler in the 1950s as a series of "rooms" enclosed by geometric box hedges, with neat topiary and square-cut hornbeams surrounding the lawn. Although I like only pink and white flowers near the house, my gardeners cleverly ensure there is changing color and interest throughout the year.

villa in a wide, west London street, surrounded by its
own garden. It's not a huge house, by any means, but
the rooms are spacious and well proportioned, with
French doors and windows letting light and flowers and
greenery almost into the rooms. So what better than to
continue the theme indoors?

Downstairs, flower-printed materials with a fairly
colorless background seem to sink into the sitting
room's extremities, and are hardly noticeable. In the
darker, more library-like living area, which is walled in
mossy green mohair velvet, with stark white-painted
doorcases and chair rail to give emphasis to the
original architecture, the florals leap forward invitingly
to accentuate and illuminate. And though the color
schemes were chosen to reflect those in a couple of
fabulously important paintings, the florals hold their
own against the art without dominating it. Waxed wood
floors, sheathed with fluffy white rugs, give the floral
exuberance a firmly natural foundation.

In the elegant drawing room *(right)*, walls painted in
a wonderfully restful "ashes of lilac" color provide a subtly
neutral background for a collection of twentieth-century
masters. Twin metal lanterns hang above the two seating
areas, their candles reflected in a pair of ivory-white antique
mirrors. The drapery material has been used for the seat
furniture in the adjoining library *(above)*, and the long sofa
has been given a structural outline by caterpillar fringing
in the pink of the Picasso painting hanging above.

STRIPE TEASE

We all know there is no end to the games stripes can play—broadening, lengthening, giving height, adding drama, subtly enclosing. As a rule, and especially in less traditional settings, I believe in the bolder, the better. Focusing on good, strong stripes can disguise many an architectural sin. For floors, where we used to have to make do with stone and wood (and remember lino?), there are now many extraordinary surfaces that have gentleness and warmth. Monotones seem to work best on a big scale, but delicate, multicolored stripes used en masse in small spaces are curiously restful.

Rooms of a different stripe from all over: an alcove in an English country house *(above left)* has been turned into an inviting seating area, with a built-in banquette covered and skirted in the same floral stripe fabric as has been used for the wall covering, drapes, and shade. The ceiling and walls of this more contemporary breakfast room in New York *(above right)* are decorated with painted stripes. The fabric covering the banquette was specially printed to line up exactly with the stripes on the walls. The wide widths of black and cream Corian flooring *(opposite)* pull together the geometric shapes in the hall and emphasize the wrought-iron stair rail.

A bedroom in a triplex on London's Park Lane *(above)* has been given a smart, masculine feel with NH Design's "Balcony Stripe" fabric in Unearthly Brown, used to line the walls and cornice, upholster the bed, and form a pleated backdrop behind it. It's simple but so chic.

"That pot should really be sitting in the center of a white stripe."

I made this sketch *(above)* of a corridor linking the main building to the indoor swimming pool for a house in Oxfordshire. Only the narrow columns, apparently holding up the awning, are real. The sepia landscape walls, Chinese fretwork railings, and darker sepia ceiling of the completed room *(right)* were painted by Paul Czainski.

High, wide, and handsome stripes bring a touch of sophistication to a child's bedroom *(right)*. Two colorways of "Shutter Stripe" (New-Mown Green and Pomegranate Red) from NH Design's "Random Harvest" fabric collection cover a triple-cushioned stool *(below)* and walls in an apartment in Monaco *(below center)*. It's fun to use this stuff in unexpected places and ways, so it looks a bit surreal.

Walls decorated with broad vertical stripes in sky-blue and white, emblazoned with plaster swags *(above, far right)*, are typical of the fearlessly camp style of Dorothy Draper at the Palácio Quitandinha, a hotel outside Rio de Janeiro (see also page 112). The carpet, with its lush, green, leafy print, brings the nearby rainforest indoors.

I can't, for the life of me, remember doing this room (*below*). Good thing, as it's a bit of a shambles, and the window is a beast to do anything with, but I like to be reminded of those sugarplum-and-white stripes of yesteryear. The octagonal bathroom (*inset, below*), with its simple, blue-striped drapes, seemed the epitome of elegance in the 1980s.

I absolutely fell in love with this red-striped *papier peint* the moment I saw it and have used it many times, most recently in a tiny spare bedroom in the Hunting Lodge (*above*). Both the bed and drapes (out of shot) have been done in a jumble of red-striped stuff; the rug beneath the Gustavian chair is actually a saddle blanket. The charmingly rustic breakfast room (*right*) and the cool, bedroom lobby on Cap Ferrat (*opposite*) show that this glorious red-striped paper that I love works absolutely anywhere.

"How chic is this marbleized cornice, painted to tone with the marvelous striped papier peint?"

The head design team—(opposite, from left), Colette van den Thillart, Lucy Derbyshire, Jena Quinn, and Ethan Paramesh—gather round me to discuss final approval of the "strikes" for our first fabric collection, named, due to its overall theme and the several sources that inspired it, "Random Harvest." Early samples stacked on shelves (left) gave us ideas as to which colors would work best in current projects. Chairs in the studio, covered in a version of an initial design (below), showed us that the black stripe was too powerful, so it was removed and renamed "After All Too," for inclusion in the edited range of the collection.

His Bright Materials

A couple of years ago, we decided to do a range of NH Design materials. My team and I had been storing up images and snippets of stuff we liked for years. The very pleasurable difficulty was boiling them down to a manageable selection.

The initial spark was the design on a nineteenth-century plate that I had found in a junk shop in North Carolina. It had, for its age, a very graphic, almost abstract representation of leaves and berries, which nudged us toward the whole collection being in the same vein: fresh and clear with hints of classical motifs. So then we had to work out the patterns and repeats, continually photocopying the originals to different scales, colors, and combinations.

Next came choosing the base cotton to print on. We wanted a fairly clean, white background, avoiding the ubiquitous cream, but stark white made the patterns dazzle the eye, and if it was grayed, they could look muddy. Eventually, we discovered a *blanc cassé* (broken white), just like the best shade of basic white paint, which gave the perfect weight and balance to the colors on it.

It was exciting when the first strike-offs came back from the printers—memories of slog and frustration vanished at seeing the real thing. Tweaking the colors and infinitesimally adjusting the scale, at last we were ready to GO with this pure, relatively simple collection. Then suddenly, from the back of a cupboard, someone pulled out the most ravishing sample, in real rocks, that the genius grotto-maker Belinda Eade had made for us several years before. Photographed, and printed on velvet, "Grotto" (see pages 72–3) became a last-minute addition, a lone star of shining brightness, in the Nicky Haslam collection, which, because of its purposely varied theme, we named "Random Harvest."

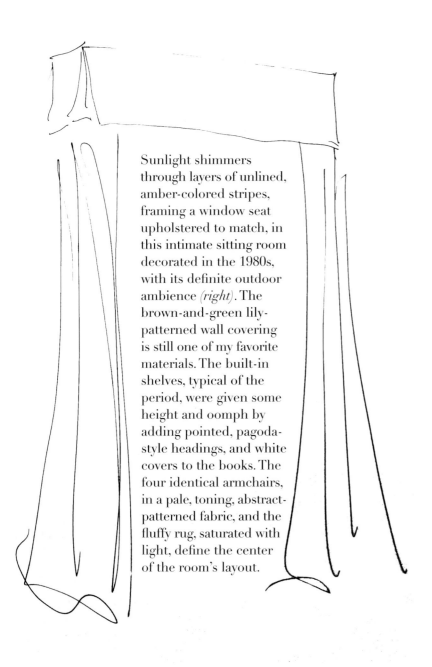

Sunlight shimmers through layers of unlined, amber-colored stripes, framing a window seat upholstered to match, in this intimate sitting room decorated in the 1980s, with its definite outdoor ambience *(right)*. The brown-and-green lily-patterned wall covering is still one of my favorite materials. The built-in shelves, typical of the period, were given some height and oomph by adding pointed, pagoda-style headings, and white covers to the books. The four identical armchairs, in a pale, toning, abstract-patterned fabric, and the fluffy rug, saturated with light, define the center of the room's layout.

CURTAIN CALLS

A s Ethel Merman sang in the 1959 Broadway musical *Gypsy*, 'Curtain up, light the lights...', it's when the lights are on that curtains come into play. I've got nothing against acres of bare glass, but with a deluge beating against it, there is nothing nicer than the soft swish of a pulled drape to transform a room into a haven, where light and shadow play on fluid flutes, glowing striations, or sculptured curves. Drapes give definition always and glamour frequently, and, without the tomfoolery of overloading, they impart a sense of wellbeing.

A tall window in a dining room in Belgravia *(left)* has a shaped, stiffened pelmet painted by Lizzie Porter in 3D "rocaille" on neutral linen. In the same apartment *(opposite)*, the paneling was glazed with several shades of muted white to accentuate the gilded moldings and the richness of the white satin, gold-tasseled, and pelmeted drapes, a scheme based on Robert Adam's amazing carved wood swags at Harewood House in Leeds *(below)*. The furniture is kept to soft grays and mauves so that the walls are the dominant feature. I used some leftover white satin to curtain the garden door at the Hunting Lodge *(below left)*, breaking the run of pinkish-terracotta cotton on the windows on either side. The wonderful curtain maker Geoff Kent of S. C. Sadler made me several of these petersham "roses" *(left)* many years ago. They are incredibly useful for covering difficult joins, or popping over pictures, if there's a hook to hide.

"Drapes, whether calm or complicated,
are like the frame of a picture."

To make the taller window dominate in this drawing room *(left)*, I decided against repeating the triple-swag treatment seen on its shorter neighbor, so as to give a cleaner line below the carved wood pelmet box. Looking at it here, I rather wish I'd put a length of simple dark fringe under it and avoided the abrupt transition from room to garden. While we were reinstating the plasterwork ceiling and walls and adding the stonework arcade to this seventeenth-century manor house in Surrey *(right)*, I did sketches *(below)* to determine the best way of disguising the fact that the windows were small and high, with radiators beneath them. Dramatic pelmets above and huge knots below, in a sort of Hampton Court style, were the starting point. I then decided on shallow benches with shaped, gadrooned backs and floor-length fringe, rather than leave the radiators exposed.

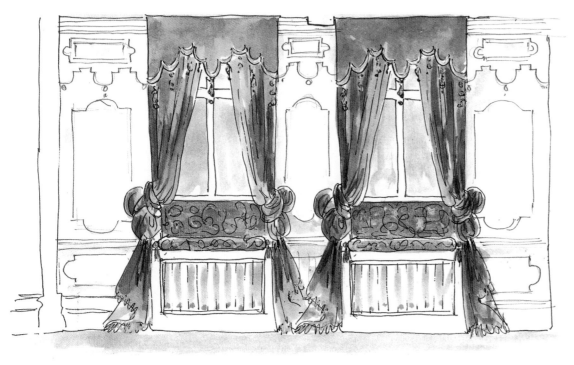

I've used my own bed's corona *(left and below)* — still as it was when John Fowler installed it — as a model many times, sometimes more elaborately but always with loose pleating and, most importantly, with a narrow band of matching stuff to define the edge. The mauve trim on this corona in Louisiana *(opposite)* brings out that color in the material, and is echoed by the stripe in the bathroom next door.

Cherry-red cotton borders the faint blue-on-white patterned lining material of the drapes and pelmets *(right)*. The pelmets are shaped to correspond to the contour of the deep window embrasures, which themselves follow the line of the windows, with their lead-latticed panes. Fowler's trick of putting strips of wallpaper border vertically and spaced regularly (start in the middle if you try this) instantly adds visual height to a room.

A hard, floating pelmet, scrolled top and bottom, for both the bed and windows *(far left)*, has a wide line of defining color on the lower edge, creating a break with the casually gathered drapes. The top scrolls create a deep shadow above them, visually dramatizing the pelmets' relatively narrow projection. In this seductive bedroom of a rock musician in London *(above)*, the deep canopy, with its lightweight gathered pelmet, hides an air-conditioning unit. Cigar-colored walls anchor the white drapes and the plaster lights on either side of the exaggerated baroque headboard. A Jacobean barley-twist bed *(left)* has the sheerest white voile falling from its dark wood cornice, avoiding any feeling of confinement in this low-beamed farmhouse bedroom.

Easily movable chairs are essential pieces for any room, especially my country sitting room *(right)*, which is a mere 12-foot square. If the chair (just seen on the far right) wasn't a cinch to move, one couldn't get to the sofas, let alone open the door to the garden. When it comes to sofas, comfort is paramount, and these ones have been with me for forty years.

The red-striped slipper chair in this bedroom *(above)* makes me smile, while reminding me of the ferny one with Elsie Mendl on page 173. A gauze-covered chair, like the one in my sketch *(right)*, often finds its way into bathrooms I design.

CHAIR COUTURE

Chairs have been designed more than any other pieces of furniture, to suit the evolving proportions of the human frame. But however hard people try to improve their design, the eighteenth-century French *menuisiers* were there first, creating shapes that fitted the giant and the child in comfort, a lady's elbow resting on an arm just so, a man's torso properly supported, the seat accommodating the clothing style of the day. With the arrival of upholstered sofas from Turkey, the "easy" chair was born, and the amalgamation of the two genres gives infinite variety to the rooms we live in today.

"Chairs can be deep and comfortable or more structured, to make you sit up and think. But, as our most essential bit of furniture, they should always look seductive."

My essential movable chairs, with slipcovers in Warner's "Fancy Lining" *(opposite)* and Colefax and Fowler's "Fuchsia" chintz *(left)* just fit into my sitting room, to provide extra seating. But be warned: when you need to have new covers made, remember to measure the chair and not the old cover, as it will have shrunk, like mine. This page *(far left)* is from a book by an almost forgotten American designer, William Pahlmann, who had some wacky ideas about chair covers.

This high-backed, casual-feeling banquette *(right)* has presence but doesn't detract from the majorly important painting above it, by Matisse. The glass-topped table is covered in velvet.

In my sketch *(left)*, the chairs with slipcovers with applied initials are dotted around a hall and a study in a Swiss chalet. But they are also easy to pull up to the dining table or use on the balcony for summer lunches, overlooking the wide-ranging landscape below.

Finding this romantic, sham-"ruin" Swedish clock in Brussels was the clue to the decoration of this turn-of-the-century dining room, near Beaulieu-sur-Mer in the south of France, with its walls lined in "Louis" paneling from the 1900s. Swedish-style chairs, with slipcovers and skirts in natural linen, surround a circular blue-and-white painted dining table, based on one I had recently seen in the Pagodenburg, the enchanting chinoiserie pavilion by the lake at the baroque Nymphenburg Palace in Munich.

My dining chairs, a steal when I bought them, have followed me from pillar to post. Covered in a classic check, with a bit of Goldfinger metallic paste rubbed on the frames *(above)*, they fit happily into the original décor of Cecil Beaton's London home during the period I rented it. Now they are at the Hunting Lodge, covered in a Pierre Frey fabric, "Ming," which depicts wonkily piled-up china bowls. Bigger checks on the backs of these chairs in a Chelsea kitchen *(opposite)* mimic the manganese Dutch tiles above the sink beyond. The leather seats and backs are hand-painted with figures in traditional Russian costume, taken from a nineteenth-century set of engravings.

*"When is a chair
not a chair?
When it's
a mile-long
Moroccan pouffe."*

This painting for an indoor/
outdoor veranda was part of
an initial scheme for a villa
outside Marrakech. We were
trying to achieve something
different from traditional "riad"
decoration, hence, the huge
plaster lanterns and the
flowing white cotton drapes,
with checkerboard borders
that continue the theme
upward from the black-and-
white tiling on the floor.

dar
Jabal al Barid
morocco

Nicholas Harlam 2008

In the library-cum-eating area at one end of the sitting room in my London apartment *(inset)*, chairs from all parts of the room can harmonize, when needed, with the four painted stools to which I subject my guests. Like many other favorite pieces, they have traveled with me from home to home for years. When not in use for dining, the table is, as here, covered in piles of books.

SIT BY ME

IN THE PAST, THERE WERE DOMESTIC CHAIRS FOR ALMOST EVERY ACTIVITY: PRAYING, NURSING, HAVING YOUR HAIR CUT, PLAYING INSTRUMENTS, MAKING GENTEEL LOVE (A *DOS-À-DOS*), WARMING BESIDE A FIRE (A *CHAUFFEUSE*, WHICH IS NOT A FEMALE DRIVER), PERCHING ON GIDDILY AT BALLS, NOT TO MENTION FOR WRITING, READING, AND INTIMATE WASHING.

Now the range has sensibly, if unromantically, narrowed, and our chairs, other than the big, squashy ones hogged by the dogs, must take on many different roles. That old set of Victorian mahogany monsters, far too many for the dining table, branch out handily into halls and, with a splash of white paint, into bedrooms or bathrooms. Contemporary chairs, while not big on comfort, immediately update the dowdiest rooms. Whatever a chair's style, use or position, it can be dressed up or down, disguised, stripped, or clothed with infinite variety.

The chairs in this dining room were designed to complement the baroque curves of the pedestal table. The ones in the kitchen across the hall vaguely echo their outline, and their colors correspond, so they can be hauled in when the table is extended.

This dining room *(opposite and above)* in a seventeenth-century Chelsea house, with double doors leading through to the family eating area in the kitchen beyond (see page 209), has a distinctly theatrical feel, largely due to the bold mix of luxe textures and colors, as well as the flamboyant shape of the table and chairs with their grandly curved backs. The rich combination of the linen upholstery, the swags of lilac silk skirting the sideboard, the patterned silk carpet, and the festoon shade, made from strips of blue and white velvet sewn together, plays against the wall paneling, painted the color of watered-down wine, the smooth marble fireplace, and the polished wood of the floor and cabinet. The glinting gilt of the candlesticks, lantern, mirror, and picture frames adds life and movement, especially at night, when the room is lit by candles.

A couple of practical yet pretty skirted vanity units, one in a Mauny-papered bathroom in the French Quarter of New Orleans *(right)*, the other in a paneled downstairs toilet in an English country house *(below)*. Simple gathered skirts such as these at once soften and warm the cool, hard quality of a marble or porcelain sink and make what can be a purely utilitarian space feel inviting.

Very long fringing makes an excellent skirt for a stool, as in my sketch of the low ottoman *(below)*. It can even be used as a cover for a radiator when attached to a narrow shelf above.

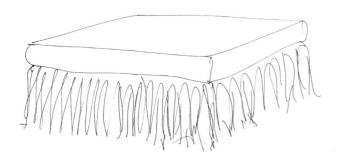

SKIRTING ISSUES

Gone are the days when people hid their bulky TV sets under a skirted table, but a cloth to the ground can still disguise a slew of unsightly paraphernalia. A draped table brings a note of informality, anchoring leggy furniture, or adding a full stop to the length of a sofa. And the cloth on a big, round library table, preferably made sturdy enough to hold piles of books, can be whipped off to create a setting for intimate suppers. Stack the books on the floor and use them—as I do, not having space for a sideboard—as surfaces for platters.

Having once seen a huge table skirted with embossed leather in the hall of the seventeenth-century Château de Haroué, each cascading fold separately inset but as supple as silk, I've always meant to copy it. On a more practical level, skirted vanity units in bathrooms or toilets relax the utilitarian confines as well as concealing any antiquated pipework and the bleach.

A horizontally striped, tailored skirt covered a rectangle of MDF in this hallway in the south of France, until we found a gilt-iron table that fits exactly over the radiator beneath (see page 96). The chic narrow edging of plain lilac reflects in the polished stone floor.

"Keep it simple; plain material, roughly gathered, does away with any hint of milady's boudoir."

The picture of me *(inset)*, was published in Nigel Dempster's gossip column in the *Daily Mail* newspaper in June, 1979. I'm wearing my idea of a maharaja's hunting uniform at my hunt-themed party, a joint celebration of my fortieth birthday and my acquisition of the Hunting Lodge (see page 47). "La Chasse" was a good theme, as it's open to many different interpretations, and it's one guys don't mind wearing. Everyone looked ravishing, from Mark Shand, dressed as a *Clockwork Orange* thug, to Rupert Everett, who was clearly an exquisitely bronzed and near-naked Masai warrior. He says that I said, "You look marvelous, darling. What have you come as? Gandhi?"

INDIAN SUMMERS

Even before my first visit there in 1986, India, with all its vibrant, colorful exoticism, has always enchanted me, so decorating this London home for a Morvi princess, where I had free rein to take the decoration to its exuberant limits, was a dream come true. Like the decadent pavilion of a maharaja, the walls of the living room *(above and right)* were swathed in lengths of fringed and tasseled off-white slub silk, and a luxurious mix of velvets and brocades in jewel-like hues of ruby and sapphire was strewn liberally over sofas, tables, and stools.

IN MY YOUTH, THE BRITISH MONARCH WAS STILL EMPEROR OF INDIA; JERKY NEWSREELS BEAMED ITS CROWDED IMMENSITY AND BEJEWELED STRANGENESS INTO MURKY CINEMAS. IN YEARS TO COME, ITS MYSTERIOUSNESS WAS TO HOLD ME IN THRALL.

When, at length, I first experienced the reality, India, as it does everyone, bowled me over. From swimming, the evening of arrival, in the Bay of Bengal via glistening follies beside lilied lakes, to the breathtaking first view of Lutyens' imperial complex in Delhi (one of only three buildings I've cried upon seeing), the country seemed like a vast, uncontained stage set crying out to be transported and rearranged.

I had the chance to achieve exactly that for the London base of an enchanting Morvi princess. From her *echt*-Art Deco palace arrived the exotic Edwardiana of a former one: state portraits, twiddly furniture, crystal, and silver. "Do your damnedest," said Uma, and not a swag or fringe, tassel, or rope was too much. Ruby and sapphire velvets echoed the ballroom-sized Aubusson carpet; emerald shades held London skies at bay; white damask gleamed. "Don't make it look too permanent," Uma had instructed. "It needs to be ephemeral." But these rooms have lasted, unchanged, for almost four decades—a tribute to the extraordinary power of Indian imagery, and imagination.

"Swathes of damask, silk, brocade, and velvet in rich, jewel-like hues conjure up the exotic opulence of a maharaja's palace."

The scheme for this opulent bedroom *(opposite and far right)* is based on hangings in the state rooms of the old city palace in Morvi, in India. At each corner of the gold-painted rattan bed are vertical wooden supports, draped in diaphanous white silk. Between them, swathes of red, blue, and gold silk are entwined with rope and tassels, with a turban of the same material crowning each post. The painted wallpaper border below the cornice echoes the swags of fabric above the bed and over the fire surround. In turn, the red-and-white striped bed covers and pillows take their cue from the striped swags on the border. The pavilion at the All India War Memorial, known as India Gate *(inset, right)*, designed by Sir Edwin Lutyens, was a foretaste of that genius architect's great masterpiece, New Delhi, which instantly moved me to tears when I first saw it.

Continuing the theme of elaborate drapery throughout the house, we hung folds of rich blue fabric, adorned with coils of thick gold rope, from the wrought-iron spiral staircase leading into the marbled hallway *(left)*. The ceiling was transformed into a tent-like canopy of pleated white silk. The paintings on the mirrored walls are from engravings of urns by the inspired eighteenth-century designer, Jean-Charles Delafosse.

Rectangles, squares, octagons, and circles form a geometric whole in this cool, bright staircase hall in a *mas* in the south of France *(left)*. I find the stylish lines of the buff-leather-covered sofa especially pleasing. The light streaming through the French doors constantly changes the silhouetted arabesques of the staircase's wrought-iron balustrade. In my garden room *(right)*, the interlooped lines of the Swedish-style chair and tripod table (the original on which my OKA design is based, see page 55) are echoed in Henry Hudson's Plasticine-and-wine-stain picture from his *Rake's Progress* series, based on Hogarth's originals. It hangs centrally above the battered old wooden writing desk that I rescued from an alley in Bordeaux.

Silhouette and Style

A good, strong profile, whether it be in architecture or furniture, is such a pleasing sensation. A combination of both—furniture that has an architectural outline—is essential for giving structure to any room. It doesn't have to be severe; arcs and curves can have the same effect, leading the eye on to and enhancing the less formal shapes. Any room needs architectural intelligence. If there's a door in one corner, put another false one in the other and the room will have an immediate structural quality; as this door won't be used, furniture can be pulled up quite close to it. Something above these doors—as large a picture as space allows, or even a few plates—will give added height.

Contrary to accepted theory, I find that big furniture will make even a small room appear larger. The same goes for ceiling lights. Let's ban the dreaded twee chandelier and have instead the most massive one possible, or a lantern. It's a good idea to have a (movable) piece of furniture under it or it'll look a bit threatening. Some interest on the ceiling, even a color, will add considerable architectural style.

SITTING STILL

Too often one sees rooms with all the seat furniture upholstered to the floor. They need a bit of leg showing, to let light through, to create shadows, to bring the whole ensemble to life. I happen to like the curved legs of European chairs above others, partly because the seats they support were designed for maximum comfort, with the frames carved to correspond exactly with the human body. All those twisty bits aren't there just for decoration; they conform to the position of the thigh, or the natural resting place for the elbow.

Simple, English-style straight legs look great in halls and libraries, even dining rooms, where a certain formal masculinity is required. Such legs don't have to be strictly "straight"— they can be architecturally inspired or have a contemporary geometry.

Lucian Freud quietly explains the subtle beauty of Watteau, one of his favorite artists, on a private visit to the Royal Academy with me *(top)*. Most of Lucian's subjects sat in this famous but raggedy leather-covered studio chair, in which James Ostrer photographed me as a Freud portrait *(above left and right)*. The picture was displayed at the National Portrait Gallery in 2001. It's fun to use odd pieces of "found" material on European chairs and run-ups, but fully upholstered chairs and sofas always seem better plainly treated, though I must admit a sneaking penchant for Dorothy Draper's batty, fringe-outlined armchairs *(right)*. Some black-and-tan African fabric, happily discovered at a market in New Orleans, was the perfect unexpected covering for this eighteenth-century French chair and stool *(opposite)*.

The Anthon Sofa *(above)*, a modern twist on a Knole design, with an apron front and kick pleats, was designed with Colette van den Thillart for the Nicky Haslam range of furniture at OKA. Silver-tasseled pillows add a note of lightness, and the ottoman/coffee table/footstool/extra seating is both practical and stylish, with its octagonal shape bringing a new dynamic to the room. The curve-seated sofa *(opposite)* was custom-made to my design for this specific space in my new apartment. The portrait of me is by Zsuzsa Furka.

"With its undulating silhouette, this is my favorite shape of sofa."

This Louis XV-style canapé *(opposite)*, covered in patterned silk in appropriately Madame de Pompadour-ish shades, would surely seduce all but the crustiest of monarchs. In the garden room at the Hunting Lodge *(below right)*, the sensuously curved sofa is covered in a splashy rose chintz. Next to it is a French canework fauteuil, with a squab covered in "Zephyr," the graduating-color ric-rac design from "Random Harvest," and a simple striped pillow. I did this painting *(below)* of an antique French ballroom sofa, now in the hall of Janet de Botton's exquisite house in Provence. Its gilt crumbling and its violet covering in tatters, the sofa is an artwork to compare with the many others its owner possesses.

A simple sketch *(above)* of the sort of elegant sofa I love. Such pieces are ideal for large entry halls and corridors, and can, of course, be made more inviting with piles of pillows.

HYDRANGEA PANICULATA: in HALL, PRADELLES, AUG 02

"Elegant antique French furniture mixes well with designs from other eras, and its design and craftsmanship is hard to beat."

MANHATTAN COCKTAIL

THIS APARTMENT IS ON THE 73RD FLOOR
OF A MAJOR NEW BUILDING IN NEW YORK.
THE BRIEF WAS TO ACHIEVE SOMETHING
VERY CONTEMPORARY BUT *VIVABLE*.

Originally, the rooms were characterless boxes, many
with floor-to-ceiling glass overlooking Central Park. They
cried out for some curves, and making the living room
oval with reflective panels, plus a swirling baroque plaster
ceiling, supplied them, besides giving more visual impact
than just the staggering view. We sheathed an off-center
structural column in Doric fluting and added a second,
hollow one, enclosing a bar and shelves. The limited
palette of silver-veined browns and bronze-greens echoes
the landscape below, mixed with the strong silhouettes
and textures of the black and white furnishings.

At one end of the living space
is a TV area *(above)*, with
facing pairs of comfortable
armchairs and a sofa in
bitter-chocolate velvet
arranged around the screen,
out of shot on the left. The
organic shape of the coffee
table echoes the curves of
the ceiling. Another seating
area *(right)*, with the dining
space beyond, is for taking in
the view. The white upholstery
reflects the sky and acts as a
foil to the earthy palette of
the enveloping caramel walls
and the bitter-chocolate and
olive-green furnishings.

Like a slash of scarlet lipstick or the glimpse of a Louboutin stiletto's crimson sole, red instantly creates a glamorous, sultry mood and brings energy to a room. The tremendous sheen of the strips of zebrawood, glazed red, which have been used to line the walls of this library-cum-study, creates a sense of decadence and luxury, which is grounded and brought into balance by the dark silvery gray rug and buttoned velvet sofa.

"Who could get any work done sitting at a desk with a view like this?"

For a table's surface, one shouldn't dismiss faux marbling. There are many skilled painters who can re-create the wonderful ancient veining and colors, not forgetting tortoiseshell, wood-graining, lacquer, and mirror. The scroll supports *(far left)* are copies of ones I saw on a church altar in Chappaquiddick, off Martha's Vineyard. The lozenge-friezed drinks table *(left)* is a good, chunky one for OKA. The lacquered top *(below)* would reflect Stephen Cornell's witty cotton-batting and paint *Jam Doughnuts* if Colette hadn't crammed it with objects. The top of the shell console table in my hall *(opposite)* is a length of painted and gilded leather, the "fringe" cut by me with scissors.

SURFACE GLAMOUR

Flat surfaces, especially console tables, look great bare but better with things on and under them—quite apart from providing essential storage opportunities. Objects, books, and lamps anchor the surfaces to the walls, and anything stashed underneath fills the void. Lots of tables have pedestals, in which case something on top, for balance, is usually necessary. That essentiality, a well-stocked drinks' tray springs to mind, but a group of objects, whether chosen for color, sentiment, or historical associations, works well, as it probably won't be moved too often.

A pair of large, semicircular half-cylinders of matte aluminum, topped with backlit glass *(this page)*, have a contemporary presence in a large Victorian apartment building with its original moldings and parquet floor. In the hallway of an apartment in Manhattan *(opposite)*, an Elliott Puckette artwork takes pride of place above an elegant gilt and metal hanging console.

I ran out of space for all my books long ago, but my slightly surreal book-table, here in my library *(left)*, opens up, so one can stash more books inside. I bought the smaller one for my garden room *(below)* and painted it white.

This shield-shaped coffee table *(right)* looks like it came off the set of a Hollywood film but, in fact, it's quite an early design, reinterpreted for OKA. Its sweeping line and tapered legs mean that it isn't too bulky or dominant in a room. Less is Henry Moore in Colette's apartment *(opposite)*, her coffee table's random curvy top and base contrasting with the nail-outlined angularity of the sofa.

"Luckily, there are books cataloging the ancient veining and colors of marble, and their beauty blows your socks off."

Having seen these gigantic fallen columns in Turkey *(above)*, I made this "ruin" dining table *(opposite)*, with a surface like a slab of hewn stone, for a tall classical portico on Cap Ferrat. It pulls apart to form two separate units. The chair covers, apparently torn, have silver thread around the "patches." An earlier devotee of faux ruins painted this octagonal antique table *(right)*.

I bought a white marble center table at auction, which was very reminiscent of those in the dairy at Rambouillet (see page 177). I had this maquette *(above)* made for future reference, as I admired the simplicity of the center column and tapered legs. This table *(right)* breaks all the accepted rules of classicism, but has arresting presence in an enfilade of tall, lacquered-doored rooms.

CANDLE GLOW

I HARDLY NEED TO GO ON ABOUT THE
CHARM OF CANDLELIGHT, EXCEPT TO SAY
THAT IT'S BEST TO HAVE AS MANY CANDLES
AS POSSIBLE, AND DOUSE THE ELECTRIC.
THERE'S NOTHING LIKE THEIR SOFT GLEAM
TO ENHANCE THE TABLE, THE GUESTS, AND
THE CONVERSATION.

For my money, candles should always be white or that
natural wax color, and never tapered or twisted. They
should look as if one always uses them, not just for a
gala occasion. Recently, wonderful fakes have come on
the market, with little batteries in them and a totally
convincing "flame" you just push on or off. They are
completely magical when dining "al fresco"—a euphemism
for the howling gale we romantics will sit through for
the unparalleled pleasure of eating out-of-doors.

This open-air Bajan rocaille pavilion
(above) is the most theatrical setting for
entertaining. The glazed stone walls glow
iridescently by candlelight, which creates
flickering shadows on the shell-festooned
arches housing stone figures. The tabletop,
on its seaweed-colored base, is a sheet of
glass backed with silver paper to re-create
the mirrored effect of the original, owned
by the Duchess of Windsor (see also pages
100–1). The reproduction Louis XVI chairs
around it have crisp, white slipcovers. The
chandelier had to have electric candles, as
the beating of tiny birds' wings snuffed
out the wax ones, but I never mind the
mix of candle- and lamplight. Now that
battery candles, such as I have at home
(inset), have become so realistic, we can
have candlelight in the stiffest of breezes.
This romantic London dining room (right)
has an old-world charm with its classically
paneled walls, marble fire surround, and
French furniture. I lit the room solely with
candles, even in the daytime, which can
often look a bit daft, but the diaphanous
pleated and gathered window treatment
gives a feeling of dusk even at noon.

I love headboards that instantly draw the eye and create drama. I found a 1920s photograph, by Milton Gendel, of Iris Origo lying on her bed in her Roman palazzo. I couldn't resist copying her baroque headboard and have used it many times. The sketch *(right)* shows it taking center stage in this scheme for a chalet bedroom. The finished room *(opposite)* shows it *in situ* against painted hessian. The romantic bedroom *(below)*, a frou-frou of Frenchified fantasy, was done for a delicious blonde, who whiled away many hours in it dreaming of being a Belle Époque courtesan.

FIELD OF DREAMS

Beds have gotten so huge these days, it's hard to know what will prevent them from looking like a football stadium. With the ubiquitous comforter, a counterpane ("bedspread" was considered fearfully common in my youth) is a bit *de trop* and unwieldy, so the best way to make a statement is with a wacky or sculptural headboard. Then there's the added problem of people wanting a vast, retractable TV inches from their toes. Though most will probably never read in bed, I always install those pinpoint lights in case, as well as "decorative" lamps on night tables, which themselves should be as large as possible, and two-tiered. Another good trick is to have a dim light source, which stays on permanently, hidden under the night table—no problems when stumbling for the Alka-Seltzer.

My father's great friend and my godmother, the writer Iris Origo *(inset)*, whose bed was the inspiration for my headboard design *(top)*.

My love affair with this vivacious style really started with the Gothick Box. This toy fort of a house *(right)* was—indeed, still is, though sadly disfigured—in a narrow lane in Chelsea. I met its owner, Simon Fleet, in the mid-1950s. His passion for all things quirky opened my eyes, while his circle of friends, Cecil Beaton among them, became mine. I found the Gothick settee *(above)* chucked out on a street in Edinburgh. Luckily, it fit in my tiny car and is now in my dining room at the Hunting Lodge. The drapes behind it have hand-painted Gothick-patterned borders. The painted Gothick chair *(above right)* in the same room is the original that inspired those in the OKA collection.

TIMELESS GOTHICK

As enduring as the Gothick style may seem now, there was a time when it hardly rated a look. People muddled the style, exemplified by Horace Walpole's eighteenth-century Strawberry Hill villa, with Gothic without a K, that heavy ecclesiastical revival so beloved of mid-Victorian architects. It was Sir Kenneth Clark, writing in his seminal book, *The Gothic Revival* (1928), on Gothick with a K that opened eyes, mine anyway. I don't see how anyone couldn't love the style. It's so lighthearted and ebullient, whether used *in toto* or just a few dashes, where the look and the style, particularly when painted and pale, fit into any room without overpowering them. But then, I live in a house with a Gothick-looking façade, so I'm *parti pris*.

The saloon at Arbury Hall in Warwickshire *(above)*, with its breathtaking plasterwork ceiling and bay window with filigree tracery, is a miracle of craftsmanship, an ecclesiastical idiom transformed into icing-sugar domesticity. The design for the room, by W. Hanwell, was approved in 1786, and work was completed in 1803. The blue and white Gothick church at Shobdon in Herefordshire *(right)*, which has a direct connection with Walpole's Strawberry Hill, makes divine worship far more divine. This is a pretty perfect re-creation by OKA of my bedroom in the country *(far right)*, featuring the Arcady Chair with a Saintclou squab.

However belligerent battlements may look on castles, when transposed to furniture, they become positively playful. This closet *(opposite)* has the whole Gothick gamut—crenellations, quatrefoils, and heraldic shields—in carved wood, and commands attention in a rustic, low-ceilinged, bedroom. My dining room's chest-on-stand *(below)* has an enchanting carved oak-leaf catch. I've adapted the pierced star-and-trefoil doors as fronts for hi-fi speakers. The Gothick proportions and detailing are evident in the cabinet I designed for OKA *(opposite, inset)*.

The oak leaf *(above left)* and trefoil, as on the "clubs" suit of traditional playing cards *(above right)*, are classic Gothick motifs found on everything from furniture, paneling, stonework, and plasterwork to fabric and wallpaper. The soaring arches and elaborate tracery, quatrefoils, and fleur-de-lis seen in Gothick churches and castles are other recurring fanciful emblems.

GREAT PRETENDERS

I dearly love things that aren't what they seem. I don't mean fakes, though I'm not against them, either. Almost any boring bit of furniture can be made more fun with some astute carved or applied details, let alone judicious paintwork. And with a bit of willpower, one can do it oneself. I made the tabletop in my dining room *(opposite, top left and right)*, by gluing some leftover tiles inside a baton frame, and "marbelizing" the painted surround with a marker pen, in about an hour.

People are awfully snotty about fake flowers, but remember, Madame de Pompadour used to have the parterres at Versailles changed with different schemes of porcelain flowers during dinner, and waited five years for a new piece of furniture with the latest finish. She'd have gone bonkers for acrylic.

This eighteenth-century chair with painted classical motifs *(left)* came from the Capri house of Mona, Countess von Bismarck, renowned for her refined taste. It is clearly a close relation of the two I saw while leafing through *Rooms* by Carl Skoggard *(above)*. I made the Russian-tiled console table in my dining room *(opposite, top)* by chopping a table in half (its counterpart is chintz-covered in my garden room). The top of the OKA sideboard *(opposite, below)* is painted to look like pale Purbeck marble. Naive scenes *(overleaf, left)*, surrounded by fantasy wood-graining and marble, enliven the doors of an Austrian "peasant" closet. The painted cupboard in my apartment is German *(overleaf, right)*. The blue trellis covers book-wallpapered doors, with real books behind. The cartridge-paper camellia was a decoration for an Inès de la Fressange fashion party.

Canadian-born Colette van den Thillart is Creative Director at NH Design, and her style perfectly complements my own. In her drawing room, the confident blend of eclectic pieces—the sinuously curved organic shapes offsetting the lines of the period architecture—and the uplifting palette inspired by nature, with earthy browns and stone balanced by fresh blues, greens, and whites, is at once modern and classic, irreverent and upbeat.

LIGHTHEARTED LUXE

THERE'S SOMETHING SO SATISFYING ABOUT
A ROOM THAT LOOKS AS IF IT HAS COME
TOGETHER OVERNIGHT, WITHOUT THE FATIGUE
OF SWATCH-AND-SOUL-SEARCHING. THESE
ROOMS, IN COLETTE VAN DEN THILLART'S
APARTMENT, WERE ASSEMBLED IN ABOUT
TWO DAYS. ALMOST ANYTHING "GOES"
TOGETHER WHEN HARMONIOUSLY PLACED.

The living room breathed a wonderful romantic
association from the moment we saw it. This was partly
because it had once belonged to fashion designers Ossie
Clark and Celia Birtwell—and was the setting for David
Hockney's portrait of them with their white cat, now in
Tate Britain—and also its location, which has a whiff of
southern Russia about it. With its stuccoed balconies
brushed by fall leaves, one could be in nineteenth-
century Odessa. When decorating it, that atmosphere
subconsciously exerted itself—the bluish walls, so like
the Wedgwood beloved by the czars, the pine-forest
green of the wood-grain carpet, the constructivist-like
stuff on the chairs, the white plasterwork, furniture, and
objects. It was a perfect example of a room "speaking,"
telling one its own preferences, guiding the hand and eye.

What appears to be an ivory-colored Empire porcelain stove in Colette's dining room *(right)* is, in fact, an Egyptian-friezed, painted-wood cupboard, its dignified contours proud against the earthy, textured background. As soon as I saw it, I immediately realized that this was how I should disguise a jumble of unsightly, non-reroutable pipes in my sitting room; having a second one built to make up a pair (and fitting it out as a bar and china cupboard), was a no-brainer (see pages 102–3). If you can't get a stove, get a cat. *Mr and Mrs Clark and Percy (above)* was painted by David Hockney in this very room between 1970 and 1971, at the height of the couple's success as dress designers and shortly after their wedding, at which Hockney was the best man. The furnishings in Colette's dining room— in shades of fresh green, pale blue, white, and chocolate in complementary striped patterns—continue the palette and mood elsewhere in the apartment.

Classical Language

I feel every room is improved by a touch of the "classical," either in furniture or an object; it brings something intellectual, something timeless. The important thing is that it must have guts, not mere dainty detailing. And the classicism can be updated, exploded even, to create whacking great scale or individual presence. There are many casts of classical elements made by museums and specialists worldwide. So there's no need to go broke on nineteenth-century copies of eighteenth-century copies of antique originals.

Outdoor things indoors look amazing. Lichened stone, mossy terracotta, and crumbly wood can stop a room from appearing sterile, and add that essential element of surprise—

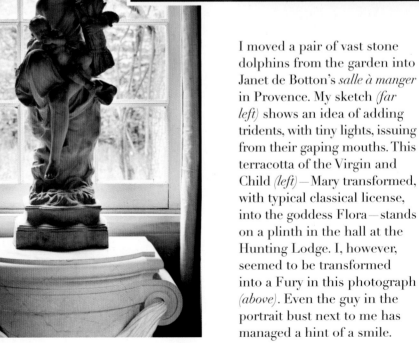

I moved a pair of vast stone dolphins from the garden into Janet de Botton's *salle à manger* in Provence. My sketch *(far left)* shows an idea of adding tridents, with tiny lights, issuing from their gaping mouths. This terracotta of the Virgin and Child *(left)*—Mary transformed, with typical classical license, into the goddess Flora—stands on a plinth in the hall at the Hunting Lodge. I, however, seemed to be transformed into a Fury in this photograph *(above)*. Even the guy in the portrait bust next to me has managed a hint of a smile.

A classical influence is evident in the design of these console tables, which bring white relief to a brown color scheme. The NH Design balustrade console *(above)* gives a less dominant effect than the chunky, marble-topped one *(top left and right)*, based on an Ionic column with a typical ram's head adorning the capital. The mussel artwork above it is by Susie MacMurray.

humor even—without the chilly cliché of more conventional marble. I know I harp on about white, but I do love the confectioners'-sugar quality of unpainted plaster and white-painted furniture. Both are so refreshing, making a sparkling contrast to darker colors and shadows around them, or melding into a cool-toned unity, without losing their intrinsic integrity and sensual silhouette.

The fireplace with a plaster urn and rope-swagged overmantel *(far left)* is the epitome of that thin 1930s classicism. I don't love it, but can see it has a period elegance. I far prefer my dumpy, lichen-encrusted stone urn *(left)*. I made some white and red coral branches from pipe cleaners to fill this cast of my favorite urn on a windowsill above a staircase *(below)*. I thumbnail-sketched the urn-shaped stove and chimney *(below left)*, plonked willy-nilly in a grand room in central Europe. I rather admire such devil-may-carelessness.

The Chimney Breast
The Grand Salon
Klosters
for Mr. and Mrs. R. W.

I love plaques every bit as much
as urns. I often use them above
fireplaces, to get away from the
clichés of mirrors or pictures.
The drawing *(above)* shows the
idea for a carved wood plaque
and fire surround for a sitting
room in Klosters. Once installed
(right), the painted plaque is as
white as snow against the warm
pine paneling. A fiberglass cast
of a metope from the Parthenon
is set into the wall above my
bathtub in London *(above right)*.
There is also an urn, naturally.

The *c*1820 painting *(below)* shows the incredible similarities of Hamilton's original design to my proposed one, with the low built-in bookcases all round the room and a collection of plaster busts. There was no way we could ignore such a coincidence, so a warm, soft, brownish red was chosen for the final scheme *(opposite, top)*.

LE TEMPS RETROUVÉ

ONCE IN A RARE WHILE, IN MY DESIGNING LIFE, AN UNCANNY COINCIDENCE HAS OCCURRED THAT HAS GIVEN ME SHIVERS DOWN MY SPINE.

This huge room, built by the assistant to Lord Elgin, contains the plaster casts (right up my street) of the Parthenon Marbles, made on site as they were taken down. When I was asked to decorate it, the frieze and black marble fire surround were the only things remaining. The walls had been stripped and graffitied, the ceiling and floor water-stained. I did a sketch with a blue scheme, suggesting bookcases, busts, and pictures, including the little one propped up beside the fireplace. Then the art historian John Harris told us he knew of a painting of the room, *c*1820. Astonishment! Apart from it being red instead of blue, the room had been almost identical to my sketch, right down to the little picture by the fireplace. Shivers department. And I did the walls red, of course.

The grand ballroom, as it was then, was added to this seventeenth-century manor house in Chelsea in the early 1800s by William Hamilton, Lord Elgin's secretary, in order to display the frieze of plaster-cast reliefs of the Parthenon Marbles that had been taken under his supervision. Since William Hamilton's time, the building had become a school, and when I first saw the space, having been asked to decorate the house by my beloved friend Natasha Kagalovsky, it had been stripped of everything but the plaster frieze and marble fire surround. My initial watercolor *(opposite, below)* shows the blue scheme that I first proposed for the room.

Mirrors over vanity units and sinks—whether hung from a bold red ribbon *(below left)* or by more conventional means—are best lit from both sides, as this gives the most flattering light. There are many styles to choose from: ornate and decorative *(left)*, sleek and modern *(below left)*, and somewhere in between *(below)*. Make sure you take into account the relevant safety laws regarding lighting in "wet" areas; other than that, the choice is yours.

It's no secret that I love to paint furniture and other pieces, either to help them fit into a scheme or simply to give them more character and individuality. This spot-spattered wall light, with its chintz half-shades, is one of a pair in my garden room at the Hunting Lodge.

Lights Fantastic

It's fun to have some visible light sources in a room, especially sconces and wall brackets, and the keynote is individuality. While there are a million perfectly nice and sophisticated lights of this sort around, a bit of rooting around in junk shops often turns up gems, which can always be painted.

The best technique for lighting pictures is to get those cheap metal ones and paint them the same color as the wall—anything to avoid that jumpy lacquered brass. If there's enough space, lights under the pictures as well, angled upward, give depth, shadow, and liveliness to walls with art massed on them, reminiscent in style of an eighteenth-century "hang."

"*Some interesting paintwork and, when needed, imaginative shades, give lights a unique twist.*"

These scroll-edged plaster wall lights are real favorites of mine, with or without shades. Bare of shades, they light the way along a landing in this chic brown and white apartment *(this page)*, and with simple, white half-shades, they pop against the glossy, dark green walls of our new office *(opposite, top right)*.

Two crystal chandeliers, hung quite low, give importance to a connecting lobby *(opposite)*, where doors on either side allow no space for furniture. I had the Giacometti-inspired lantern made for my sitting room *(this page)*. It's even bigger than it looks, but so airy that it doesn't dominate. Ian Bishop, who actualized my design from copper tubes and gypsum-soaked bandages, could stand upright inside it before it was hung.

The pared-down designs of
French interior designer
Jean-Michel Frank *(right)*, both
futuristic and taken from nature,
have influenced decoration
ever since he created them.
These large, shell-like discs
are among the most beautiful
ceiling lights imaginable,
seen here in Colette van den
Thillart's dining room *(above)*.

Grand vase chinois en staff. Alberto
Giacometti, 1937.
Large chinese vase in staff. (Alberto
Giacometti.)

Vase en terre cuite orné latéralement d'un
entrelac. Alberto Giacometti.
Terra cotta vase with tracery on the
side. (Alberto Giacometti.)

Grand vase abstrait en staff
Giacometti, 1936.
Large chinese vase in staff. (Alberto
Giacometti, 1937.)

Vase-bilboquet en staff. Alberto Giacometti,
1937.
Cup and ball vase in staff. (Alberto
Giacometti, 1937.)

and Diego Gi

Vase en terre cuite. (Diego Giacometti.)
Terra cotta vase. (Diego Giacometti.)

Plafonnier à pointes, en staff. (Diego Giacometti, 1937).
Pointed ceiling lamp in staff. (Diego Giacometti, 19

Suggestion en staff, inspirées par des patelles.
(Alberto Giacometti, 1936).
Staff hanging lamps inspired by patella. (Alb
Giacometti, 1936).

Plafonnier spirale, en staff. Diego Giacometti, 1936).
Spiral ceiling lamp in staff. (Diego Giacometti, 1936).

I imagine the design for this glorious lamp *(above)*, its stand formed as an oversized tassel, dates from the 1940s. I had some made after seeing them in a friend's *quinta* outside Rio de Janeiro. Here, it beautifully illuminates the folds of the pleated blue fabric lining the walls and the ruched-velvet edge of the elaborate antique Venetian headboard. A pair of 1920s porcelain lamps stand at each end of a chest of drawers in this chalet bedroom *(above right)*, their softly gathered floral shades throwing a gentle light over the antique mirror on the wall behind. The decorative metal wall light above, casting shadowy patterns onto the beamed ceiling, also dates from the 1920s. This lamp, with its pretty shade of pleated antique Mauny wallpaper *(right)*, stands on a narrow end table that I designed, in the "old" hall at my Hunting Lodge, which I use as another sitting room, especially in the winter. It is illuminating a picture of a sphinx by Martin Battersby.

DARKER HOURS

I OFTEN WONDER HOW MANY PEOPLE USE ALL THE MOOD-SETTINGS THEY HAVE INSTALLED WITH THOSE ELABORATE PROGRAMS THAT CONTROL THE LIGHTING. I IMAGINE, LIKE ME, THEY FIND A COUPLE OF VARIATIONS THAT SUIT THEIR, AND THE ROOM'S MOOD, AND LEAVE IT AT THAT.

Having overhead and wall lighting on one circuit, and table lamps on another, seems to do the trick without all that fumbling. (Unless, of course, there is some fumbling in the offing, when the best plan is to have as little light as possible.) Pools of soft light on tabletops and a gleam from an unseen source are ideal in a romantic evening setting, restful to the eye, and can be integrated with a couple of brighter beams for reading and working—always remembering that the light should fall over the left shoulder for the right-handed and vice versa. And, of course, bright but fairly concentrated lights for bedside tables, plus those snaky pinpoints for small-hours reading, are essential. It seems that no one in mainland Europe reads in bed. A weak, yellowish glow (probably from those horrid, long-lived filaments) is about all one can hope for. I always travel with a couple of old-fashioned 60-watt light bulbs.

For a while, my London base was an apartment in an unprepossessing, just-post-war building—German bombs having obliterated the original Victorian mansions on the site—opposite the Natural History Museum. There is a theory that if Hitler had won the war, he intended to make that museum his palace, so maybe such pinpoint shelling was a dry run for making a suitable parade ground. The apartment was in an extremely convenient location, but in the building's basement and, therefore, fairly dark. I thought the only thing to do was to make it darker, while leaving the typical "period" cornice-concealed light track. I made the walls a dark prune color, with a flecked silver-mica ceiling. Almost all the pieces of furniture I had from previous places miraculously fit in, their pale surfaces and dramatic shadows creating a sense of perspective in the warm glow. These were clearly not rooms designed for daytime living, but after office hours or a weekend in the country, they were easy, mellow spaces for entertaining or chilling.

Personal Gestures

The dearth of junk shops, these days, is depressing. Gone is the time when every country town, indeed village, had a shop where one might find, if not a treasure, at least some attractive trash. "Nice young men who sell antiques," as Noël Coward sang in "Lets do it," now cluster into provincial "centers" or put stuff up on eBay. But that doesn't stop me swinging into anywhere with a sign saying "Antiques," though most of them only sell that gift-shop junk or repro Sheratondale. Nor can I resist the lure of a flea market. One just may find something that gives a room, table, or wall that all-important personal touch.

Often I've inadvertently started people on a quest for a collection. I don't mean anything grand, but prints, plates, or bronzes. I found a wonderful rope chandelier for a house in the south of France the other day, and then, by chance, a jug modeled

Rummaging in market stalls, as I am in Vienna *(above)*, is always a lure, but sadly less and less likely to produce the odd prize that will delight friends or clients for its appropriateness. The huge black-and-white of Cupid up to his usual tricks—an amusing theater flat for some forgotten 1930s revue—completely covers one wall in Colette's sitting room *(above left)*. Wacky touches such as this diffuse the seriousness, creating a playful and highly personal atmosphere.

On a higher scale, while rifling though the catalogs of auction houses and salerooms worldwide, one often sees something that shouts out where and to whom it should belong. This eighteenth-century, German, gilt-framed mirror was clearly destined for the hall in this chalet.

The owners of this study, with its black marble fireplace *(left)*, had many engravings and prints of Irish views and figures. The plan was to reframe them, but realizing their dark wood and ebonized frames counterbalanced the black below, we hung the huggermugger like this. The way in which objects are displayed can give them a sense of status, as with this set of china *(above)*.

as coiled rope and a set of French engravings of intricate knots. At once, the room had a theme, a gesture to understated unity.

I have unwittingly collected anything to do with children playing games. It started, I now see, years ago, when I found four gently colored, dog-eared engravings of Italian urchins playing Blind Man's Bluff, Grandmother's Footsteps, and the like. A Bordeaux flea market came up with a print of tots in elaborate eighteenth-century clothing fooling around on stilts, and in St Petersburg, one of children slithering down an ice hill. Now friends send me versions of the subject from all over the world.

Among the many rewarding and inspiring periods of my career, my partnership with Paolo Moschino is the most memorable. We found we both had the same approach to decoration, and it was encouraging to see his sure hand and eye helping to create these cool, light-filled rooms, incorporating, yet again, many of the same possessions that have always been my staples. His branch of our design business has gone from strength to strength, and I am as proud of my initial input as I am of his continued originality and highly regarded talent.

ENDURING ELEMENTS

NOTHING IS MORE SATISFYING THAN BEING ABLE TO USE FAVORITE PIECES OF FURNITURE ONE HAS HAD FOR EVER IN NEW AND DIFFERENT SETTINGS.

The rooms on these four pages were done by Paolo Moschino and me several years ago. Even then, many of the pieces had had a previous incarnation, and have gone on to be used in other, more recent, and even current, situations. Perhaps the most amazing of these old friends is the pair of banquettes *(opposite)*. I designed them nearly three decades ago, and I've somehow jammed them into everywhere I've lived since, including my new apartment (see pages 278–83). Even more astonishing is that they still have their original gray-beige linen slipcovers, which were a steal at the time and have never worn out.

The classical Swedish-y bed *(below)* has also moved to subsequent quarters (see page 104). I painted it a sludgy green originally, but then did it off-white, and it has stayed that color ever since. Several other pieces have, likewise, traveled with me, to be used, rejigged, or

refreshed, to suit their various new positions. I love that continuum; the ongoing presence of these pieces in my life has such a pleasing and anchoring effect on me, to say nothing of being thrifty.

The big artwork, in its Jean Cocteau-like frame *(opposite)*, is a special treasure. I'd seen, at the home of a great collector, Pauline Karpidis, a tiny Salvador Dalí sketch of classical ruins framed by Cocteau in gold. It was one of the most enchanting objects imaginable, and unique. Pauline, very sweetly, allowed me to make this much larger version. It now hangs, embedded in faux marble, above the fireplace in the sitting room of my new apartment, its presence constantly reminding me of the original and its fascinating owner.

These simple objects *(left)*, grouped together on a suede tabletop, were mostly found in flea markets. A wicker lamp *(below)*—now in the Hunting Lodge—stands on a console in front of a lithograph set (the artist's proofs) of parakeets, by Elizabeth Butterworth. The four stools, with covers painted to look like a "Picasso" when they're pushed together—see my original design *(below left)*—and Jean Cocteau's profile *(opposite)* take on a different persona in each rearrangement.

Here and Now

Well, the title says it all. After a lifetime of looking and lusting, I've found the living space I've always desired: one huge ground-floor room, with a couple of bathrooms and bedrooms. It has high ceilings, good plasterwork, hardwood floors, and a fireplace of warm, amber-colored marble—the ideal bones on which to put decorative flesh. I wanted the whole place to look lighthearted, almost transient, with nothing precious—but rather, frankly, fake.

All the decorative threads of a lifetime are finally drawn together in my sitting room *(left and above)*, its simple, cartoon-style paneling and faux marble overmantel painted by Karen Morris, the oak floor whitened, the distance blued, the layout spacious. An etching by Tracey Emin hangs above Cecil Beaton's ink-drawing of Chanel *(left)*.

My beloved friend Prue Penn gave me the portrait of herself, painted at the height of her astonishing beauty. I matched the walls of the library/dining area to the blue of her stole, and made the room vaguely octagonal by reusing the trelliswork panels that had been in the windows of my former design studio near Sloane Square.

Then the charm and the fakes: the electric coal fire, in a fire basket from my childhood home; the battery-operated candles in gilt-bronze holders; the garden chairs; the overscale Giacometti-inspired lantern; the pair of "Swedish stoves" (one is a drinks cabinet, the other masks a multitude of gas and water pipes). The best fake of all is a pair of "porcelain" eagles on brackets above the mantel. In fact, they are plastic bird-scarers from my local hardware shop, sprayed white with car paint.

I find I want every book published, so as well covering my dining table, books are stashed in bookcases hidden by a white-book trompe l'oeil wallpaper behind the trellis panels *(above and opposite)*. I'm far too lazy to put them in any order, so I just shove them in at random and the whole muddle is hidden from view. The Warhol-esque portraits of me to the right of the fireplace *(opposite)* are by Skid Stewart.

"That there are antique things here from my childhood and other pieces bought yesterday, makes being in this room both nostalgic and vividly current."

I got the grand piano, a rare, 100-year-old Broadwood made of Brazilian mahogany, on eBay for $425. Yes, and it was in almost-perfect tune; it's not even a fake. The girandoles on either side of the window belonged to Nancy Mitford when she worked at Heywood Hill's bookshop in Curzon Street.

Two garden chairs flank the fireplace, next to the old banquettes. The fire basket, now with an electric fire, is from Hundridge. In front, the white wood column reminds me of those huge fallen ones in Turkey. The "porcelain" eagles perch on brackets on the faux-marble overmantel, lit by battery candles in candlesticks that belonged to my parents.

PICTURE CREDITS

The author and publisher would like to thank the following photographers and agencies for their kind permission to reproduce the photographs in this book.

Unless otherwise specified, all illustrations and watercolors are by Nicky Haslam, and all other images are from Nicky Haslam's personal collection or the NH Design Archive.

Author's note: My library grows daily and there are so many books that I turn to frequently for guidance, advice, amusement, nostalgia, and inspiration, in the hope that a little of the consummate creativity found therein will be transmitted to my own endeavors. Images from some of these publications are included in this book, with my grateful thanks.

Pages: 2 Simon Upton; **3** Simon Upton/The Interior Archive; **6–7** John Swannell; **9** Simon Upton/The Interior Archive; **10** Simon Upton/The Interior Archive; **14–15** *Country Life* © IPC Media; **15 below left and below right** *Country Life* © IPC Media; **16 top left and top right** Simon Upton © Jacqui Small; **17** Painting by John Hookham photographed by Simon Upton © Jacqui Small; **18** *Country Life* © IPC Media; **19** *Country Life* © IPC Media; **20** Painting by John Hookham photographed by Simon Upton © Jacqui Small; **21 top** *Country Life* © IPC Media; **21 inset** *Dream of St Ursula*, 1495 (tempera on canvas), Carpaccio, Vittore (c1460/5–1523/6)/ Galleria dell'Accademia, Venice, Italy/Cameraphoto Arte Venezia/Bridgeman Images; **22 top left** Painting by John Hookham photographed by Simon Upton © Jacqui Small; **22 inset top right** Vita Sackville-West, 1927 (b/w photo), English Photographer, (twentieth century)/Private Collection/Bridgeman Images; **22 inset center** Architect, Geoffrey Scott, by Hugo Ritter von Bouvard, 1925/RIBA Library Drawings & Archives Collections; **23 top right** Painting John Hookham photographed by Simon Upton © Jacqui Small; **26 top left** Painting by Michael Wishart photographed by Dylan Thomas © Jacqui Small; **26 top right** *Daily Mail*/Solo Syndication; **27 below left** Painting by Michael Wishart photographed by Dylan Thomas © Jacqui Small; **27 top right** Painting by Nicky Haslam photographed by Dylan Thomas © Jacqui Small; **27 below right** Painting by Kate Kinsella photographed by Dylan Thomas © Jacqui Small; **29 top left** Andy Warhol and Diana Vreeland by Ron Galella/ Getty Images; **30 top left** Taken from *In the Pink—Dorothy Draper (America's Most Fabulous Decorator)*, Carleton Varney, Pointed Leaf Press; **30 top right** Bruce Davidson, Michael Ochs Archive, *Vogue* 1962; **30 center** "Baby" Jane Holzer at the Peppermint Lounge, Michael Ochs Archives; **32 center** *House & Garden* © Condé Nast Publications Inc.; **36 below right** Richard Young/REX, Berkeley Square Ball, 10 April 1979, David Bailey, Lord Lichfield, and Nicky Haslam; **37** Fritz von der Schulenburg/The Interior Archive; **38–9** Fritz von der Schulenburg/The Interior Archive; **40** Fritz von der Schulenburg/Interior Archive; **41 left** Simon Upton © Jacqui Small; **41 top right** Fritz von der Schulenburg/The Interior Archive; **42 top** Fritz von der Schulenburg/The Interior Archive; **43** Fritz von der Schulenburg/ The Interior Archive; **44 top** Artwork photographed by Simon Upton © Jacqui Small; **44 below** Christopher Simon Sykes/The Interior Archive; **45 left and right** Simon Upton © Jacqui Small; **46 top and center** Christopher Simon Sykes/The Interior Archive; **46 below** Taken from *Intorno dalla Tavola* by Rosita Adamoli, Illustrati Mondadori; **47 top left** Christopher Simon Sykes/The Interior Archive; **48** Michael Nicholson/*The World of Interiors* © Condé Nast Publications Ltd; **49 below right** David M. Benett/Getty Images Entertainment; **50 below** Richard Young/REX; **52 top** Taken from *Preussische Königsschlösser in Berlin und Potsdam* by E. A. Seemann; **54** Fritz von der Schulenburg/*The World of Interiors* © Condé Nast Publications Ltd; **55 top right, center, and below** Nick Pope, OKA; **56 below right** Christopher Cormack/Corbis; **61 below left** David M. Benett/Getty Images Entertainment; **65 top right** Image from Richard Buckle's The Diaghilev Exhibition at Forbes House, 1954, decoration and sculptures designed by Leonard Rosoman and executed by Peter Lyon; **65 below left** Taken from *Tony Duquette 1950s/60s*, by Wendy Goodman and Hutton Wilkinson, Foreword by Dominick Dunne, Abrams; **66 below right** Richard Young; **73 top right** Michelle Carangi; **73 background fabric** "Grotto," inspired by Belinda Eade; **76** Simon Upton © Jacqui Small; **77** Simon Upton © Jacqui Small; **78–9 and 79** Simon Upton © Jacqui Small; **81** Andrew Twort/*Architectural Digest* © Condé Nast Publications Inc.; **82** Fritz von der Schulenburg; **83** Fritz von der Schulenburg; **84 top and center** Fritz von der Schulenburg; **85** Fritz von der Schulenburg; **86–7** Andrew Twort/*Architectural Digest* © Condé Nast Publications Inc.; **88 below left** Fritz von der Schulenburg/*The World of Interiors* © Condé Nast Publications Ltd; **89** Simon Upton; **90 and 91 top** Simon Upton © Jacqui Small; **91 below** Dylan Thomas © Jacqui Small; **92 left** Fritz von der Schulenburg/The Interior Archive; **92 top right** Andrew Wood; **92 below right** Fritz von der Schulenburg/The Interior Archive; **92 below center** Taken from *In the Pink—Dorothy Draper (America's Most Fabulous Decorator)*, Carleton Varney, Pointed Leaf Press; **93 below right** Taken from *Requisitioned—The British Country House in the Second World War*, John Martin Robinson, Aurum Press; **96** Simon Upton; **97** Fritz von der Schulenburg/*The World of Interiors* © Condé Nast Publications Ltd; **98 top right** Simon Upton; **98 top left** Dylan Thomas © Jacqui Small; **98 bottom** Taken from *Elsie de Wolfe—A Decorative Life*, Nina Campbell, Aurum Press; **99** Simon Upton; **100** Fritz von der Schulenburg/The Interior Archive; **101 below left** Fritz von der Schulenburg/The Interior Archive; **101 center right** Taken from *Horst Interiors* by Barbara Plumb, Bulfinch; **102 and 102–3** Simon Upton © Jacqui Small; **104 and 104–5** Simon Upton © Jacqui Small; **106** Fritz von der Schulenburg; **106 inset** Dylan Thomas © Jacqui Small; **107** Fritz von der Schulenburg; **108 and 108–9** Gerardo Jaconelli; **110 top** Derry Moore; **110 inset** *Country Life* © IPC Media; **111** Derry Moore; **112 top left** Fritz von der Schulenburg; **112 center and right** Taken from *In the Pink—Dorothy Draper (America's Most Fabulous Decorator)*, Carleton Varney, Pointed Leaf Press; **112 below right** Fritz von der Schulenburg; **113** Fritz von der Schulenburg; **114** Simon Upton © Jacqui Small; **115 top right** Andrew Wood; **115** "Shutter Stripe" photographed by Dylan Thomas © Jacqui Small; **115 below left** Simon Upton; **116 top** Fritz von der Schulenburg/The Interior Archive; **116 center** Catherine II, the Great (1729–1796)/Universal History Archive/UIG/Bridgeman Images; **116–17** Andrew Twort/ *Architectural Digest* © Condé Nast Publications Inc.; **118 below** Taken from *The Age of Baroque in Portugal*, Jay A Levenson, National Gallery of Art, Yale; **118–19** Andrew Twort/*Architectural Digest* © Condé Nast Publications Inc.; **120** Simon Upton; **121 below** Simon Upton; **121 below left and right** Simon Upton © Jacqui Small; **122 below** *The Fête at Rambouillet or, The Island of Love*, c1770 (oil on canvas), Fragonard, Jean-Honoré (1732–1806)/ Fundaçao Calouste Gulbenkian, Lisbon, Portugal/Giraudon/Bridgeman Images; **123** Simon Upton © Jacqui Small; **124–5** James Fennell/*House & Garden* © Condé Nast Publications Ltd; **125 below right** James Fennell/*House & Garden* © Condé Nast Publications Ltd; **125 top right** Fritz von der Schulenburg/The Interior Archive; **125 below left** *The Swing* (oil on canvas), Fragonard, Jean-Honoré (1732–1806) (after) Musée Lambinet, Versailles, France/Giraudon/Bridgeman Images; **128** Simon Upton © Jacqui Small; **128–9** Simon Upton © Jacqui Small; **130** Evgeniya Luchina; **131 right** David Montgomery, *Sheer Opulence*, CICO Books; **131 center** b p k/Bildagentur für Kunst, Kultur und Geschichte; **132** Simon Upton © Jacqui Small; **133** Simon Upton © Jacqui Small; **134–5** Simon Upton; **135 top left** *Rouen Cathedral, Sunrise*, 1825 (oil on millboard), Bonington, Richard Parkes (1802–28)/Minneapolis Institute of Arts, MN, USA/The Sheila C. and John L. Morgan Endowment for Art Acquisition/Bridgeman Images; **135 below right** *Portrait of the Marchesa Luisa Casati with a Greyhound*, 1908 (oil on canvas), Boldini, Giovanni (1842–1931)/Private Collection/Photo © Christie's Images/Bridgeman Images; **136–7** Simon Upton; **138–9** Simon Upton; **140 top left** Gerardo Jaconelli; **140 top right** © Conde Nast Publications Inc.; **140 below left** *Two Foot Flowers*, 1964 (silk screen inks and synthetic polymer on canvas), Warhol, Andy (1928–87)/Private Collection/Photo © Christie's Images/Bridgeman Images; **140 below right** *Shoes*, 1980 (synthetic polymer, diamond dust, and silk screen inks on canvas-un), Warhol, Andy (1928–87), Bayerische Staatsgemaeldesammlungen—Museum Brandhorst Munich; **141** Simon Upton © Jacqui Small; **142 below right** Dylan Thomas © Jacqui Small; **143** Andrew Twort/*Architectural Digest* © Condé Nast Publications Inc.; **144 below right** Simon Upton © Jacqui Small; **145 top left** Simon Upton © Jacqui Small; **145 right** Simon Upton/The Interior Archive; **146 left and right** Andreas von Einsiedel/*House & Garden* © Condé Nast Publications Ltd; **147** Andreas von Einsiedel/*House & Garden* © Condé Nast Publications Ltd; **147 inset** Diana Cochrane; **148 and inset** Simon Upton © Jacqui Small; **149 and inset** Simon Upton © Jacqui Small; **150 top** Andrew Twort/*Architectural Digest* © Condé Nast Publications Inc.; **150 center** Harry Cory Wright; **150 below** Andrew

Wood; **151 top right** Simon Upton/*The World of Interiors* © Condé Nast Publications Ltd; **151 below left** Simon Upton/*The World of Interiors* © Condé Nast Publications Ltd; **152** Simon Upton © Jacqui Small; **153** Simon Upton © Jacqui Small; **154 top left** Evgeniya Luchina; **154 inset center** Elena Topler; **154 inset top right** John Swannell; **155** Simon Upton/*The World of Interiors* © Condé Nast Publications Ltd; **156** Evgeniya Luchina; **157** Evgeniya Luchina; **158** Simon Upton © Jacqui Small; **159** Simon Upton © Jacqui Small; **160 and 160–1** Fritz von der Schulenburg; **162** Andrew Wood; **163** Andrew Wood; **164** Andrew Wood; **165** Andrew Wood; **166–7** Dylan Thomas © Jacqui Small; **168–9** Simon Upton; **170–1** Fritz von der Schulenburg/*The World of Interiors* © Condé Nast Publications Ltd; **172** Simon Upton; **173 top left** Taken from *Elsie de Wolfe—A Decorative Life*, Nina Campbell, Aurum Press; **173 center and below right** Derry Moore; **174–5 and 175** James Fennell/*House & Garden* © Condé Nast Publications Ltd; **176** Simon Upton/*The World of Interiors* © Condé Nast Publications Ltd; **177 top right** Simon Upton; **178** Simon Upton; **179** Simon Upton/*The World of Interiors* © Condé Nast Publications Ltd; **180–1** Derry Moore; **180 inset** Simon Upton © Jacqui Small; **182 and 182–3** Derry Moore; **184 top left** Derry Moore; **184 top right** Simon Upton © Jacqui Small; **184 below left** John Paul; **185** Fritz von der Schulenburg; **186 below right** Andrew Twort/*Architectural Digest* © Condé Nast Publications Inc.; **187 top left** Fritz von der Schulenburg; **187 below left** Gerardo Jaconelli; **187 below right** Taken from *In the Pink—Dorothy Draper (America's Most Fabulous Decorator)*, Carleton Varney, Pointed Leaf Press; **188 top left** Simon Upton © Jacqui Small; **188 center** Andrew Twort/*Architectural Digest* © Condé Nast Publications Inc.; **188 top right** Simon Brown/*House & Garden* © Condé Nast Publications Ltd; **188 below right** Derry Moore; **189** Derry Moore/*Architectural Digest* © Condé Nast Publications Inc.; **190** Simon Upton © Jacqui Small; **191** Simon Upton © Jacqui Small; **192–3** Simon Brown/*House & Garden* © Condé Nast Publications Ltd; **194 top left** David Montgomery, *Sheer Opulence*, CICO Books; **194 below left** Simon Upton © Jacqui Small; **194 below right** Christopher Simon Sykes/The Interior Archive; **195** David Montgomery, *Sheer Opulence*, CICO Books; **196 top** Andrew Twort/*Architectural Digest* © Condé Nast Publications Inc.; **198 top left** Simon Upton © Jacqui Small; **198 below left** Simon Upton; **199** Andrew Wood; **200–1** Andrew Twort/*Architectural Digest* © Condé Nast Publications Inc.; **201 top** Fritz von der Schulenburg; **201 below** Simon Upton; **202 top left** Derry Moore/*Architectural Digest* © Condé Nast Publications Inc.; **202–3** Simon Upton/The Interior Archive; **204** Simon Upton © Jacqui Small; **205 top left** Taken from *The Pahlmann Book of Interior Design*, William Pahlmann; **205 top right** Simon Upton © Jacqui Small; **205 center** Derry Moore; **206–7** Derry Moore/*Architectural Digest* © Condé Nast Publications Inc.; **208** Andreas von Einsiedel/*House & Garden* © Condé Nast Publications Ltd; **209** Simon Upton/*The World of Interiors* © Condé Nast Publications Ltd; **212** Simon Upton/*The World of Interiors* © Condé Nast Publications Ltd; **213 right** Simon Upton/*The World of Interiors* © Condé Nast Publications Ltd; **213 inset** Simon Upton/The Interior Archive; **214 top right** Simon Upton; **214 below left** Simon Upton; **215** Simon Upton/The Interior Archive; **216 and 216–17** James Mortimer/*The World of Interiors* © Condé Nast Publications Ltd; **218** James Mortimer/*The World of Interiors* © Condé Nast Publications Ltd; **219 top right and below left** James Mortimer/*The World of Interiors* © Condé Nast Publications Ltd; **220** Simon Upton/The Interior Archive; **221** Simon Upton © Jacqui Small; **222 below right** Taken from *In the Pink—Dorothy Draper (America's Most Fabulous Decorator)*, Carleton Varney, Pointed Leaf Press; **223** Gerardo Jaconelli; **224** Nick Pope, OKA; **225** Simon Upton/The Interior Archive; **226 below right** Simon Upton © Jacqui Small; **227** Simon Brown/*House & Garden* © Condé Nast Publications Ltd; **228 inset** James Osterer; **228 and 228–9** Simon Upton © Jacqui Small; **230–1** Simon Upton © Jacqui Small; **232 top left** Simon Upton/The Interior Archive; **232 center** Nick Pope, OKA; **233** Simon Upton © Jacqui Small; **234** James Mortimer/*The World of Interiors* © Condé Nast Publications Ltd; **235** Simon Upton © Jacqui Small; **236 top left** Simon Upton © Jacqui Small; **236 center** Simon Upton © Jacqui Small; **236 below right** Nick Pope, OKA; **237** Simon Upton © Jacqui Small; **238** David Montgomery, *Sheer Opulence*, CICO Books; **239 top left** Fritz von der Schulenburg/The Interior Archive; **239 top right** Fritz von der Schulenburg/The Interior Archive; **239 below left** Dylan Thomas © Jacqui Small; **239 below right** John Paul; **240** Fritz von der Schulenburg/The Interior Archive; **240 inset** Simon Upton/The Interior Archive; **241** Simon Brown/*House & Garden* © Condé Nast Publications Ltd; **242 below** Simon Brown/*House & Garden* © Condé Nast Publications Ltd; **243 top** Fritz von der Schulenburg/*The World of Interiors* © Condé Nast Publications Ltd; **244 top left** Simon Upton © Jacqui Small; **244 top right** Simon Upton © Jacqui Small; **244 below right** Simon Upton © Jacqui Small; **245 top** Roman von Gotz/Arcaid/Corbis; **245 below left** Edwin Smith/RIBA Library Photographs Collection; **245 below right** Nick Pope, OKA; **246** Simon Upton; **246 inset** Nick Pope, OKA; **247 below left** Simon Upton; **247 below center** Quercus (w/c and gouache over pencil on vellum), Conyers, Matilda (1753–1803)/Private Collection/Photo © The Maas Gallery, London/Bridgeman Images; **247 below right** Playing card: Jack of Clubs (color litho), American School (nineteenth century)/Dallas Historical Society, Texas, USA/Bridgeman Images; **248 top left** Simon Upton; **248 top right** Taken from *Rooms*, Carl Skoggard, Rizzoli; **249 top left and right** Simon Upton © Jacqui Small; **249 below** Nick Pope, OKA; **250** Fritz von der Schulenburg/*The World of Interiors* © Condé Nast Publications Ltd; **251** Simon Upton © Jacqui Small; **252–3** Simon Upton © Jacqui Small; **253 inset** David Hockney, photo-collage *George, Blanche, Celia, Albert and Percy*; **254 inset** David Hockney, *Mr and Mrs Clark and Percy* 1970–1, Acrylic on canvas 84 x 120in © David Hockney, Collection Tate, London; **254–5** Simon Upton © Jacqui Small; **256 top right** Jude Edginton; **256 below center** Simon Upton © Jacqui Small; **257 top left and right** Simon Upton © Jacqui Small; **257 inset** Fritz von der Schulenburg; **258 inset** Taken from *In the Pink—Dorothy Draper (America's Most Fabulous Decorator)*, Carleton Varney, Pointed Leaf Press; **258 top right** Simon Upton © Jacqui Small; **258 below right** Fritz von der Schulenburg; **259 top right** Simon Upton/The Interior Archive; **259 below right** Fritz von der Schulenburg/*The World of Interiors* © Condé Nast Publications Ltd; **261 top** Simon Upton/*The World of Interiors* © Condé Nast Publications Ltd; **261 inset** Simon Upton © Jacqui Small; **262 top left** Fritz von der Schulenburg/*The World of Interiors* © Condé Nast Publications Ltd; **262 top right** Simon Upton © Jacqui Small; **262 below left** Fritz von der Schulenburg; **262 below center** John Paul; **262 below right** Simon Upton © Jacqui Small; **263** Fritz von der Schulenburg; **264** Andrew Wood; **265** Simon Upton © Jacqui Small; **266 top and inset left** Simon Upton © Jacqui Small; **266 below center and right inset** Taken from *Jean-Michel Frank—Adolphe Chanaux*, Léopold Diego Sánchez, Éditions du Regard; **267 top left** Gerardo Jaconelli; **267 top right** Fritz von der Schulenburg/*The World of Interiors* © Condé Nast Publications Ltd; **268** Simon Upton/The Interior Archive; **269** Simon Upton/The Interior Archive; **270 left** Simon Upton © Jacqui Small; **271** Fritz von der Schulenburg/*The World of Interiors* © Condé Nast Publications Ltd; **272–3** James Fennell/*House & Garden* © Condé Nast Publications Ltd; **273 right** Simon Upton; **274** Simon Upton/The Interior Archive; **275** Simon Upton/The Interior Archive; **276** Simon Upton/The Interior Archive; **277** Simon Upton/The Interior Archive; **278–9 and 279** Simon Upton/The Interior Archive; **280** Simon Upton © Jacqui Small; **281** Simon Upton/The Interior Archive; **282** Simon Upton © Jacqui Small; **283** Simon Upton/The Interior Archive.

Jacket credits

Front cover: Simon Upton/The Interior Archive.
Back cover: Top row, left to right: Dylan Thomas; NH Design Archive; Simon Upton; Christopher Simon Sykes; NH Design Archive; Simon Upton; NH Design Archive; **Bottom row, left to right:** James Fennell/*House & Garden* © Conde Nast Publications Ltd; Simon Upton; Richard Young; NH Design Archive; Derry Moore; Simon Upton; Nick Pope.

Every effort has been made to trace the copyright holders. We apologize in advance for any unintentional omissions and would be pleased to insert the appropriate acknowledgment in any subsequent editions.

INDEX

This book is dedicated to Candida Lycett Green